REVELATIONS OF GLORY

Prayers for Saints' Days

DAVID ADAM

kevin mayhew

kevin mayhew

First published in Great Britain in 2017 by Kevin Mayhew Ltd
Buxhall, Stowmarket, Suffolk IP14 3BW
Tel: +44 (0) 1449 737978 Fax: +44 (0) 1449 737834
E-mail: info@kevinmayhew.com

www.kevinmayhew.com

9 8 7 6 5 4 3 2 1 0

ISBN 978 1 84867 891 0
Catalogue No. 1501543

Cover design by Rob Mortonson

Typeset by Angela Selfe

Printed and bound in Great Britain

Contents

April

May

June

July

August

September

October

November

December

About the author

David Adam was the Vicar of Lindisfarne, off the Northumbrian coast, for 13 years until he retired in March 2003. His work involved ministering to thousands of pilgrims and other visitors. He is the author of many inspiring books on spirituality and prayer, and his Celtic writings have rekindled a keen interest in our Christian heritage. For details of all David Adam's books published by Kevin Mayhew, please see our website: www.kevinmayhew.com.

Introduction

When St Paul writes to the church in Corinth he describes them as 'called to be saints' (1 Corinthians 1:2). He had no illusions about the church there, he was well aware of their problems and their failures. He knew what they were like but he also saw the potential of what they could be: they were called to be saints. They were called to be the people God had made them to be and to do what God had called them to do. They were not called to be someone different but to be different in their way of living, for they were called to reveal God's glory in their midst.

The lives of saints are not different from other human lives. They have the same joys and sorrows, the same struggles and temptations. The saints are not set apart as perfect or sinless, for they have the same weaknesses as all humans. They are not people that spend most of their time in church or on their knees in prayer, but they are who God has called them to be. They are themselves, and in being themselves they reveal God's glory. By the way they live, they show God's love, compassion, peace and powers to renew and recreate. They are people who work in common union with God and he is seen at work in their lives. Such lives are a challenge to us. They question where our priorities lie, our attitude to God's world and to each other; they make us look at our attitudes towards life and possessions and make us ask what is truly precious to us.

In our present world, saints are hardly remembered by the majority of Christians; they are no longer our guides or our heroes. We do not celebrate their days or know much about them. Yet, we have become festival hungry and have to invent other things to celebrate. There is a danger we create our heroes only from television stars or from sport. It is good to see people we would like to be like, but we must remember we are called to be ourselves and not a poor copy of someone else. Use your heroes to inspire you, but to do what you feel you are called to do. This book is to introduce you to some of the people who are heroes of the Church and are revelations of God's glory. We share a common union with them, for we have the same Creator and Redeemer and the same Spirit of God: in God, we are one with them. You are called to be one with the saints, so live up to your calling.

Each celebration of a saint begins with a short introduction to the saint's life, hoping it will encourage you to find out more. Then the readings for the saint's day are taken mainly from the Common Worship Lectionary as used by the Church of England, the Scottish Episcopal Church, the Church in Wales, and other churches within the Anglican Communion. This is very close to the Common Lectionary of the Roman Catholic Church, and is used by other denominations. An opening prayer or 'collect' – that is, a prayer to help us collect and centre our thoughts – is after the readings. Then come the intercessions, an offering of the peace, and the blessing. All this could be used for a short service in a house group or in your home.

Remember intercessions do not belong to the priests and ministers alone, but are very much your sharing in the prayers of the Church. The intercessions follow the pattern of many books of prayer: we pray in turn for the Church, the world, our homes and loved ones, for the sick and the needy, and finally we remember the communion of saints and the departed. If you add the readings from the Lectionary to the prayers, spending some time in quiet and meditation, it will transform your worship at home and in church, and it will transform you also. Use this book as a means of opening up to the presence of God. May God help you to see that you are a means for revealing his glory.

Intercession is a good way to share with God all that is in your heart, knowing that it is already in God's heart, so your heart and his heart are one, you abide in him and he abides in you. Often intercession is an opening of our heart to God and so getting a glimpse of glory. I believe that deep intercession begins in the heart. Go out from your prayers knowing that God is in your heart and in the hearts of all that you meet; return to your prayers with all that you have met and experienced in your heart to be joined to the heart of God. It is amazing how many situations are suddenly washed with a new brightness when we know that God is there and that God cares. Do remember that silence after any petition is important. If you are leading intercession, give people space to hold the prayer before God in love and to add their own. Though I have offered a few ideas for each section, make them your own, and perhaps slim them down so that there is more time for silence and being aware of God's love.

Together with its companion volume *Icons of Glory,* this book seeks to encourage you to explore the common union to which we all belong and to discover God's call to you which is unique. This is a call to be a fellow worker with God and to reveal his glory in your life.

JANUARY

2 JANUARY

Basil the Great and Gregory of Nazianzus

Basil of Caesarea (c.330–79) and Gregory of Nazianzus (329–89) became friends while they were studying in Athens. After this for a short time Basil became a monk in Syria and in Egypt. Then he became a hermit where Gregory also came to be a hermit. Both preached to the people. In 364 Basil left his hermitage to defend the Church against the Arian emperor Valens. In 370 Basil was made Bishop of Caesarea. Just before his consecration, he distributed his inheritance to the poor and served food to the hungry. He continued to champion the Church against Arian heretics and against secular encroachment into church affairs. Basil appointed his friend Gregory as Bishop of Nazianzus in Cappadocia, where Gregory's father had been the bishop.

Readings

Proverbs 4:1-9
2 Timothy 4:1-8
Matthew 5:13-19

Opening prayer

O God of light and love, we give you thanks and praise for calling Basil and Gregory to proclaim the Good News and give witness to your presence. Grant, O Lord, that we may show your light and love to others by the way we live: through Jesus Christ our Lord.

Intercessions

O God of light and love, we remember before you all who have given their lives to show your salvation as revealed in Jesus Christ.
We give you thanks for St Basil and St Gregory and for their stand against false teaching and encouraging people to stay firm in the faith.

We ask your blessing upon all who teach the faith and on all preachers of the word.
We pray especially for those whose lives are at risk for standing firm in what they believe.
Lord of love, hear us,
and let your light shine upon us.

O God of light and love, we bring before you all who make decisions for the wellbeing of nations and people.
We pray for all who are in control of power, and all who are in government.
Lord, bless all who work for justice, fair dealings and freedom of individuals.
We remember those who seek to bring peace and unity between peoples and nations.
Lord of love, hear us,
and let your light shine upon us.

O God of light and love, may we show your light in our daily lives.
Through you, O Lord, may our homes be full of love and peace.
We remember before you all homes where there is little love, and homes where families are under stress and strain.
We pray for children who feel unloved or unwanted: and all who are taken into care.
Lord of love, hear us,
and let your light shine upon us.

O God of light and love, we remember all whose lives are darkened.
We bring before you all who are seriously ill and those awaiting operations: we pray especially for . . .
We ask your blessing upon all whose lives are in danger through violence or war.
We remember all who are hungry or homeless, and all refugees.
Lord of love, hear us,
and let your light shine upon us.

O God of light and love, as we rejoice in your gift of eternal life, we pray for our loved ones departed, especially today for . . .
With St Basil and St Gregory and all your saints, may they rejoice in life eternal.
Merciful Father,
accept these prayers for the sake of your Son, our Saviour, Jesus Christ. Amen.

The peace

Trust in God; pour out your hearts to him, for he loves you with an everlasting love. The peace of the Lord be always with you.
And also with you.

Blessing

May Christ, who sends us out, be known to be with us to strengthen and to guide us: and the blessing of God Almighty, the Father, the Son and the Holy Spirit, be upon you and remain with you always.
Amen.

12 JANUARY

Aelred of Rievaulx

Aelred was born in Hexham in 1109, the son of a parish priest. After being taken into the service of King David of Scotland, he joined the Cistercian order at Rievaulx. In 1143 he was made the abbot of Revesby and then abbot of Rievaulx. Aelred was known for his energy and his gentleness towards all. He became well known for his writing, including *The Mirror of Charity* and *Our Spiritual Friendship*. During his time as abbot of Rievaulx, the number of monks rose to 600. He is often called 'The St Bernard of the North': he began his writings at the request of St Bernard of Clairvaux. Aelred died in 1167.

Readings

Ecclesiasticus 15:1-6
Philippians 3:7-14
Luke 12:32-37

Opening prayer

Good Lord, you gave to Aelred the Abbot of Rievaulx a deep sense of brotherly love and a desire to lead others to a love of you. Teach us that it is through love that we dwell in you and you are in us. We ask this in the love of Jesus Christ our Saviour.
Amen.

Intercessions

Loving Lord, we give you thanks for all who have given their lives in the building up of your Church.
Today we give thanks for religious communities and their work of prayer and in caring for others.
We pray for the Cistercians and for communities we know, especially . . .

We remember all who offer hospitality, run retreats, and teach the faith, and those who care for the sick and poor of our world.
God of goodness and love,
hear us and help us.

Loving Lord, we pray for all who keep our local communities going through their work and dedication.
We pray for all in local government, for shopkeepers, for those who run clubs and care for our meeting places.
We remember our local doctors, care homes and emergency services, the firemen and women, paramedics and drivers of ambulances, and the work of the police.
God of goodness and love,
hear us and help us.

Loving Lord, we give thanks for our friends who have enriched our lives by their sharing with us.
We ask your blessing upon them and upon our homes and families.
We remember all who live alone and those who feel lonely and unwanted.
We pray for home visitors and befrienders.
God of goodness and love,
hear us and help us.

Loving Lord, we remember all who have stood by us and supported us in times of need.
We ask your blessing upon all who are ill, those who have been taken into care and for all who are refugees.
We remember before you friends and loved ones who are ill, especially . . .
May we who are healthy be a strength to those who are in weakness.
God of goodness and love,
hear us and help us.

Loving Lord, we rejoice in your friendship and love and know that it is everlasting. We pray for friends and loved ones departed, and pray especially for . . .
Merciful Father,
accept these prayers for the sake of your Son, our Saviour, Jesus Christ. Amen.

The peace

Know you are never alone, for your God is with you and he loves you with an everlasting love.
The peace of the Lord be always with you.
And also with you.

Blessing

Abide in God's love, allow his peace to enfold you and his presence to protect you: and the blessing of God Almighty, the Father, the Son and the Holy Spirit, be upon you and remain with you always.
Amen.

13 JANUARY

Hilary of Poitiers

Hilary was born at Poitiers into a prosperous pagan family in 315. His family saw that he got a good education. Hilary married and had a daughter. After much studying, he was baptised when he was 30. In 350 he was elected Bishop of Poitiers and got caught up in the Arian controversy. Because of his gift as an orator, he was known as the Athanasius of the West. He wrote *On the Trinity* against the Arians. Though sounding severe in some of his writings, he was known to be kind and gentle. He was a hymn writer. He had some influence on Martin of Tours. Hilary died in 368.

Readings

Isaiah 28:23-29
1 John 2:18-25
John 8:25-32

Opening prayer

Lord God of creation, we thank you for all who have defended our faith against all that would lead us astray. Following the example of Hilary, may we learn to express our faith in word and in actions, that we may be able to stand firm through your power and presence: we ask this in the love of Christ our Lord.

Intercessions

Faithful and loving God, we thank you for St Hilary and all who have been moved by the Gospel to give their lives in the service of others. We pray for those who have shared their faith with us and been an example to us. We pray for all clergy, especially for . . .

We ask your blessing upon all who are being persecuted for their faith, or who are mocked and sidelined.
We pray that we may have the courage to stand up for what we believe.
God, our light and our salvation,
hear us and help us.

Faithful and loving God, we give thanks for the gift of music, for hymn writers and all who produce music we enjoy.
We pray for all musicians, choirs and those who teach music, and those who bring music and song to our communities. We pray especially for . . .
We ask your blessing upon all who bring music into our lives and for those who bring music to people who are ill or in care.
We pray also for those who work for the freedom and acceptance of others.
God, our light and our salvation,
hear us and help us.

Faithful and loving God, we give you thanks for those who encourage us to sing and to lift up our hearts.
We ask your blessing upon our families and our friends.
We remember areas of our communities where there is oppression or depression.
We pray for communities that have been involved in some sort of disaster: we pray especially for . . .
God, our light and our salvation,
hear us and help us.

Faithful and loving God, we ask your blessing upon all who are troubled in mind or spirit, all who struggle with doubt or darkness.
We remember those who are struggling with their lives or personalities.
We pray for all who will not accept help or forgiveness, and for those who cannot forgive themselves.
We remember all who are ill at home or in hospital and we pray especially for . . .
God, our light and our salvation,
hear us and help us.

Faithful and loving God, as we give thanks for the life of St Hilary, we pray for all our loved ones who are departed from us. We pray especially today for . . .
Merciful Father,
accept these prayers for the sake of your Son, our Saviour, Jesus Christ.
Amen.

The peace

God's peace be upon you for he has called you out of darkness into the light of his glory.
The peace of the Lord be always with you.
And also with you.

Blessing

Be strong and fear not, for the Lord is steadfast in his love towards you. He is your strength, your stronghold and your shield: and the blessing of God Almighty, the Father, the Son and the Holy Spirit, be upon you and remain with you always.
Amen.

17 JANUARY

Antony of Egypt

Antony was born in Egypt at Coma c.251. When he was 20 he sold all his possessions, giving the money to the poor. He then went to live in the desert, where he sought to put the love of God before all else. He lived a life of great simplicity, making his living by making mats and gardening. Gradually he attracted like-minded disciples. From 286 to 306, Antony lived in complete solitude. He left it to guide the disciples who had gathered around him. For them he produced a simple rule of discipline and prayer. This rule had a strong effect throughout the Christian world. People looked to the 'Desert Father' for guidance and inspiration on how to live a Christian life. Antony asked to be buried in an unknown place in the desert. This was done at his death in 365. But five years later his relics were found and taken to Alexandria. Carvings of Paul and Antony, the founders of monasticism, were often placed on Celtic High Crosses, such as the one at Ruthwell in Scotland c.750.

Readings

1 Kings 19:9-18
Philippians 3:7-14
Matthew 19:16-26

Opening prayer

Father, we give you thanks for St Antony and for his willingness to stand alone to tell of your love and your glory. He chose to live a simple life, having given his money to the poor. Help us to live simply that others might simply live. We ask this in the name of him who gave his life for us, Jesus Christ our Saviour.
Amen.

Intercessions

Lord, giver of all, we rejoice in life and all that you have given to us.
Help us not to hoard or to squander what we have been given.
As we give thanks for St Antony, we ask that your Church may show that its true riches are the people it is able to bring to know your love.
At all times we pray that the Church may witness to what is important in life and that true and lasting riches are only found in you.
We ask your blessing on all who have become monks, nuns and hermits, those who live in communities that seek to show your love and care for all.
God of love and compassion,
hear our prayer.

Lord, giver of all, we remember before you all who are trapped in a consumer society, and all who are snared by the desire for more and more possessions.
We ask your blessing upon the world's poor. We remember those who do not receive a just and fair wage, and all who suffer from profiteering.
We pray for all who are kept in need through others' greed.
We ask your blessing upon the work of Fair Trade, Christian Aid, CAFOD and all relief agencies.
God of love and compassion,
hear our prayer.

Lord, giver of all, we thank you for our homes and our food and all who care for us.
We ask your blessing on homes that are seeking to make space for a time of stillness and of listening to each other.
May we always make room to hear and help where we can.
May our families, our community, our church all be known for their generosity and care.
God of love and compassion,
hear our prayer.

Lord, giver of all, we remember those who suffer through war, or climatic changes; those who have lost their land or their homes.
We pray for all who suffer from malnutrition and all who do not have clean water available.

We remember all who are ill with no one to care for them, or where there are no resources to help them.
In a moment of silence, we pray for friends and loved ones we know who are in ill or in need . . .
God of love and compassion,
hear our prayer.

Lord, giver of all, we thank you for the witness of all your saints. We remember especially today the Desert Mothers and Fathers and give thanks for their wisdom and their contribution to life.
We pray for the saints and for friends and loved ones departed;
we remember today especially . . .
Merciful Father,
accept these prayers for the sake of your Son, our Saviour, Jesus Christ.
Amen.

The peace

Know that God's presence,
God's kingdom,
God's love,
God's peace
are always at hand.
The peace of the Lord be always with you.
And also with you.

Blessing

The mighty God protect you;
the loving God enfold you;
the Spirit of God guide you:
and the blessing of God Almighty, the Father, the Son and the Holy Spirit, be upon you and remain with you always.
Amen.

19 JANUARY

Wulfstan

Wulfstan (c.1009–1095) was born of Anglo-Saxon parents at Long Itchington in Warwickshire. After his ordination in 1038 he spent 25 years in the Benedictine monastery at Worcester. Much against his will, he was elected Bishop of Worcester in 1062. He proved to be a good pastor and visited his diocese in a systematic manner. Working with Lanfranc, he helped to achieve the abolition of the slave trade between Bristol and Viking Ireland. He proved to be a good administrator and helped in Church and state during the transition period from Anglo-Saxon to Norman rule. He died on this day in 1095.

Readings

1 Samuel 16:1, 6-13
1 Corinthians 4:1-5
Matthew 24:42-46

Opening prayer

God, we give you thanks for all who have served you through the Church. We remember today Wulfstan who became Bishop of Worcester and used his talents as a pastor in the care of his diocese and his visiting every parish. As he encouraged the building of churches, help us to build up the Church in our day: through Jesus Christ our Lord.

Intercessions

Father God, we give you thanks for the Church throughout the world.
We ask your blessing upon each congregation and all who reach out in compassion towards others.
We pray for all who have pastoral duties and ask your blessing upon the Bishop of Worcester and all in the diocese. We pray for our church and all who minister.

We ask your blessing on all who seek to build up the Church in ways of justice and peace.
We remember churches that are struggling to survive and where there is little pastoral care.
Loving God,
hear our prayer.

Father God, we ask your blessing upon our world community.
We remember areas of unrest and fear and all distressed peoples.
We pray for all who work to build up community life and encourage acts of mercy and care.
We remember all who have been forced to work for low wages or are held as slaves.
We pray for those who have been forced out of their homes and country.
Loving God,
hear our prayer.

Father God, as we have richly received, help us to richly give.
We remember all who supply us with our daily needs of food and protection, and ask your blessing upon them.
We pray for all who influence the minds and hearts of people through the press and other media.
We ask your blessing upon our homes, our loved ones and those with whom we work.
Loving God,
hear our prayer.

Father God, we remember all who do medical research.
We ask your blessing upon friends and loved ones who are ill, or struggling with troubles. We pray especially for . . .
Keep us aware of those in our own communities that are in need of support and help.
We pray for those who can no longer look after themselves.
Loving God,
hear our prayer.

Father God, we give thanks for St Wulfstan and all the faithful departed.
We remember all who have been bereaved this week, especially . . .
We pray for all who have died recently, especially . . .
Merciful Father,
accept these prayers for the sake of your Son, our Saviour, Jesus Christ.
Amen.

The peace

God is with you on every journey.
God's light is there in the darkness.
God's love is there enfolding you.
The peace of the Lord be always with you.
And also with you.

Blessing

God, whose power is in all things, is with you.
God, whose presence shines in all creation, is with you.
God, whose love enfolds all, enfolds you:
and the blessing of God Almighty, the Father, the Son and the Holy Spirit, be upon you and remain with you always.
Amen.

21 JANUARY

Agnes, child martyr

Agnes was 13 years old when she was made a martyr in Rome. She is reputed to have refused an arranged marriage because of her dedication to Christ. She suffered among the last persecutions of Diocletian in about the year 304. Her bravery and resilience were among the qualities that were much admired. Her emblem in art is the lamb, as in Latin it is a play on the name *agnus,* meaning lamb.

Readings

Wisdom 4:10-15
Revelation 7:13-17
Matthew 18:1-7

Opening prayer

Lord of life and love, we remember all young people who have suffered violence or death for their faith, praying especially today in thanksgiving for St Agnes. May her faithfulness and trust in Christ be an example to us all: through him who is our Saviour, Jesus Christ our Lord.
Amen.

Intercessions

Lord of love, in times of trouble may your Church reveal to us your presence and your peace.
May the Church reach out in compassion for the poor and oppressed.
We remember all who are being persecuted for their faith, especially . . .
We ask your strength for all whose faith is being mocked or stifled by others.
Loving Lord,
hear us and help us.

Lord of love, we remember all who work to relieve the suffering of children.
We think of those who have been separated from loved ones, and families torn apart.
We pray for the work of the Children's Society, Save the Children and the NSPCC.
We ask your blessing upon all places of education and where children are cared for.
We pray for the work of the Red Cross and all who work in areas of disaster.
Loving Lord,
hear us and help us.

Lord of love, we give you thanks for those whom we love and all who love us.
We pray for our community and all groups that meet to nurture the wellbeing of children, especially . . .
We pray for all who freely give of their time to care for our community.
We ask your blessing upon children in homes that are struggling.
Loving Lord,
hear us and help us.

Lord of love, we remember all children who live on the streets of our world, especially those whose lives are endangered.
We pray for children who are taught to steal, or to be professional beggars.
We ask your blessing upon those who have no school to go to and have little protection.
We remember all who are ill and pray especially for . . .
Loving Lord,
hear us and help us.

Lord of love, we give thanks for the life and witness of St Agnes and for all your saints in glory. We ask your blessing upon friends and loved ones departed. We pray especially today for . . . that they may rest in peace and rejoice in your glory.
Merciful Father,
accept these prayers for the sake of your Son, our Saviour, Jesus Christ. Amen.

The peace

In darkness of unknowing, when love seems to have departed,
the Lord comes to you to enfold you in his love,
and to bring you the light of his presence and his peace.
The peace of the Lord be always with you.
And also with you.

Blessing

The eye of God be upon you,
the hand of God protect you,
the love of God enfold you.
God keep you from evil, shield you from harm:
and the blessing of God Almighty, the Father, the Son and the Holy Spirit, be upon you and remain with you always.
Amen.

24 JANUARY

Francis de Sales

Francis was born in 1567 in the Château de Sales in Savoy. As a student he was educated in Paris and in Padua. Though he could have had a career in law, he wanted to be a priest. He was ordained in 1593. He was soon known as a skilled preacher and as someone who cared for the poor. His preaching against Calvinism, beginning soon after his ordination, helped to win the Chablais province back to Roman Catholicism, which endangered his life. He preached with love, gentleness and patience. He was elected coadjutor-bishop of Geneva in 1599 and moved to Annecy to administer the diocese: he became its bishop in 1602. Among his most famous writings are *The Introduction to the Devout Life* and the *Treatise on the Love of God*. He died at Lyons in 1622 and his body was translated to Annecy in 1623.

Readings

Proverbs 3:13-18
1 Corinthians 2:1-10
John 3:17-21

Opening prayer

God our Father, as you called Francis de Sales to show that prayer and meditation are for all your people, help us to be faithful in prayer and lead a life that reveals its devotion to you. May we show your steadfast love and compassion to all whom we meet. We ask this in the name of Christ our Saviour.
Amen.

Intercessions

God of grace and goodness, we thank you for Francis de Sales and for his writing on prayer in the Devout Life and writing on the Love of God.

We ask your blessing upon all who speak and preach in your name, especially upon . . .
We remember the work of retreat houses and religious communities.
We pray for all who witness to your love through their own devotion.
We pray for the church to which we belong, that it may show your love and care for the community in which it is placed.
Lord, as you have created us,
hear us and help us.

God of grace and goodness, we give thanks for all who show mercy and compassion in their dealings.
We pray for those who reach out to help those in difficulties, and all relief agencies.
We remember all the homeless and displaced persons of our world and ask that they may find justice and compassion.
We ask your blessing upon those who leave their homes to care for people involved in natural disaster, or war.
Lord, as you have created us,
hear us and help us.

God of grace and goodness, we give thanks for and pray for our homes and the communities to which we belong.
We pray for any who have recently moved into our area; may we show them friendship and a welcoming hand.
We remember any who live on their own and need some care or attention.
We give thanks and pray for all who through their dedication keep local organisations and services available.
Lord, as you have created us,
hear us and help us.

God of grace and goodness, we give thanks and pray for all doctors and nurses and for our local hospitals.
We remember all who are ill at home or in hospital; we pray especially for . . .
We ask your blessing upon all who are fearful and anxious about the future or what is happening in their lives.

Lord, be strength to the weak, give hope to those in darkness, and be known to each in their needs.
Lord, as you have created us,
hear us and help us.

God of grace and goodness, as we rejoice in the life of Francis de Sales, we pray that we may learn from your saints who are now in glory. We remember all our loved ones and pray they may rejoice in the fullness of life eternal. We remember those who have died this week; we pray especially for . . .
Merciful Father,
accept these prayers for the sake of your Son, our Saviour, Jesus Christ. Amen.

The peace

Grace, goodness and peace from God,
who loves you with an everlasting love.
The peace of the Lord be always with you.
And also with you.

Blessing

The great and gracious God guide you,
that you may walk gently upon the earth,
live in peace and be compassionate to all:
and the blessing of God Almighty, the Father, the Son and the Holy Spirit, be upon you and remain with you always.
Amen.

26 JANUARY

Timothy and Titus

Timothy and Titus were companions and fellow workers with St Paul. Timothy was born of a Gentile father and a Jewish mother, and he studied the Scriptures as a young man. Paul had him circumcised to make him acceptable to the Jewish Christians (Acts 16:3). He was a representative of Paul to the peoples of Corinth, Ephesus and Thessalonica. In the letter of Paul to Timothy, he directs him to appoint bishops and deacons. Tradition has it that he was martyred by pagans when he opposed their festivals. Titus, a Gentile, was Paul's secretary for a while. He took part in the Council of Jerusalem and was sent to Corinth on a difficult mission, then was sent by Paul to Crete and later still to Dalmatia. From there he returned to Crete and is said to have been the first bishop there. He died in Crete. In Paul's letter to Titus, he is instructed to ordain presbyters and to govern the Cretans with firmness.

Readings

Isaiah 61:1-3a
2 Timothy 2:1-8 or Titus 1:1-5
Luke 10:1-9

Opening prayer

Lord God, as we rejoice in those who built up your Church by the proclaiming of the Good News, we give you thanks and praise for the lives of Timothy and Titus who were fellow workers and partners with St Paul. May we follow their example by working together in fellowship and peace to strengthen the church in our area. We ask this in the name of Christ the risen Lord.

Intercessions

Loving Lord, we ask your blessing upon the Church throughout the world.

May we remember with gratitude all who have proclaimed the Good News and shared their faith with others.
We give thanks for those who taught us of your love and saving power. May our church be one of outreach and fellowship.
We ask your blessing upon all who teach Religious Education and all those in theological colleges.
God our Saviour,
hear us and help us.

Loving Lord, we give thanks for all who give their lives in the service of others.
We ask your blessing upon all who are striving to bring peace and unity to our world.
We remember the work of the emergency services and the social services. We pray especially for . . .
We pray for all who work among the poor and outcasts of our world.
God our Saviour,
hear us and help us.

Loving Lord, we give thanks for all who have helped us to develop our talents and abilities.
We ask your blessing upon our homes and all who have nurtured us, and pray for our families and friends.
We pray for homes where there is little encouragement or communication.
We remember homes where there is a breakdown of relationships.
God our Saviour,
hear us and help us.

Loving Lord, we pray for all who feel trapped or frustrated in life and have no one to help or guide them.
We remember those who feel they have wasted their lives and talent and seek guidance.
We ask your blessing upon those who cannot continue their work through illness or circumstance. We pray also for their families and loved ones.
We remember all who are ill, and we pray especially for . . .
God our Saviour,
hear us and help us.

Loving Lord, we rejoice in the fellowship of Timothy and Titus and all your saints in glory.
We pray for our loved ones departed and for those who have died this week: we pray especially for . . .
Merciful Father,
accept these prayers for the sake of your Son, our Saviour, Jesus Christ.
Amen.

The peace

Grace and peace from God our Father and the Lord Jesus our Saviour be known in your life.
The peace of the Lord be always with you.
And also with you.

Blessing

God's goodness, God's grace, God's guidance are his gifts to you:
and the blessing of God Almighty, the Father, the Son and the Holy Spirit, be upon you and remain with you always.
Amen.

28 JANUARY

Thomas Aquinas

Thomas Aquinas (c.1225–74) was a Dominican friar and a theologian. He has been described as 'the greatest thinker in the medieval Church'. He was born at Rocca Secca near Aquino in Italy. He was educated from the age of five to thirteen at the Benedictine monastery of Monte Cassino and then at the University of Naples. In Naples he met the Dominicans; admiring their intellectual work, he set his heart on joining them, which did not please his parents. He joined the Dominicans in 1244. He imparted his learning through his writing and preaching, through the *Summa Theologica* which is still an authentic statement of Christian doctrine, and also through homilies and the writing of many hymns. He became known as the 'angelic doctor'. He died whilst on his way to the Council of Lyons in 1274.

Readings

Wisdom 7:7-10, 15, 16
1 Corinthians 2:9-16
John 16:12-15

Opening prayer

Lord God, who gave to Thomas Aquinas such wisdom and zeal for holiness, we thank you for his writings, hymns and preaching. By his example, may we be inspired to give ourselves more fully in love and service to you: we ask this through our Lord and Saviour Jesus Christ.
Amen.

Intercessions

God Almighty, may we seek to know more of your grace and goodness. May your Church be provided with faithful teachers that we may rejoice in your love and your salvation.

We ask your blessing upon all preachers of the Word, and upon those who teach others ways to pray. We pray especially for . . .
We pray for all who are new to the faith and seeking to learn, also remembering those who have grown weary in their faith and no longer seek to know more of your love.
Lord God of our salvation,
hear our prayer.

God Almighty, we ask your blessing upon world leaders and all who make momentous decisions about our future.
We pray that all may be aware of the preciousness of every creature and the balances important to life.
We pray for areas of the world that are being destroyed and wasted by greed and thoughtlessness.
We ask your blessing upon all who work in conservation and the care of our world.
Lord God of our salvation,
hear our prayer.

God Almighty, we thank you for all who have been our guides and teachers and those who have shared their vision of life.
We pray for our homes and loved ones and for all who have helped us to grow in love and life.
We ask your blessing upon the communities to which we belong and those who service them and provide us with our needs.
We remember before you all who are new to our community and also those who live among us but feel not part of our fellowship.
Lord God of our salvation,
hear our prayer.

God Almighty, we ask your blessing upon all who are seeking to discover newness in life.
We remember all who have lost their vision of the glory that is theirs.
We pray for all who are jaded with life or are despairing.
We pray for all who feel thwarted by illness or disability and for those who have the care of them.
We pray for all who work in medical research, and for those who work to relieve suffering.

We pray for friends and loved ones who are suffering in any way.
Lord God of our salvation,
hear our prayer.

God Almighty, we give thanks for the vision and dedication of Thomas Aquinas.
We rejoice that in our Saviour you have prepared a place for us in your kingdom.
We pray for all the faithful departed and our loved ones in your glory.
We pray especially today for . . .
Merciful Father,
accept these prayers for the sake of your Son, our Saviour, Jesus Christ. Amen.

The peace

God in his wisdom guide you and bring you to his peace.
The peace of the Lord be always with you.
And also with you.

Blessing

God be a guiding light to you,
a mighty strength to protect you,
a loving Lord to enfold you:
and the blessing of God Almighty, the Father, the Son and the Holy Spirit, be upon you and remain with you always.
Amen.

30 JANUARY

King Charles I

Charles Stuart was born in 1600, the second son of King James I. He became the heir apparent on the death of his brother. He came to the throne in 1625, where he came up against an increasing power of Parliament. When this was combined with the Puritans in power, and in Parliament, a Roman Catholic was sure to find life difficult. He tried to stand firm against these two powers and often dismissed sittings of Parliament and tried to enforce high-church Anglican practices, throughout England and Scotland. Opposition resulted in the Civil War which led to his defeat, imprisonment, trial and execution on this day in 1649. He remained proud to the end and his personal faith was never in doubt.

Readings

Ecclesiasticus 2:12-17
1 Timothy 6:12-16
Matthew 16:24-26

Opening prayer

God our ruler and guide, as we remember how King Charles stood firm for what he believed and died for his faith, we pray that we may be faithful in our witness. May we strive to build up the unity of your Church: we ask this in the name of our Saviour, Jesus Christ.
Amen.

Intercessions

Holy and Strong One, we remember all who seek to witness to your love and compassion under difficult circumstances and in dangerous places.
We pray for Christians being persecuted for their faith and those whose lives are in danger.

We ask your blessing upon all who seek to heal divisions and to bring peace and unity to the Church and to the world.
We pray for our own church, that it may be free of all that divides it.
Lord, in you we trust:
hear us as we call to you.

Holy and Strong One, we ask your blessing upon Elizabeth our Queen and all the members of the royal family.
We pray for leaders of nations and countries, especially where there are divisions and troubles at this time.
We remember communities and areas where there are prejudice and narrow-mindedness.
We pray for people who are forced into a way of life that they do not feel comfortable in.
Lord, in you we trust:
hear us as we call to you.

Holy and Strong One, we thank you for all who have shown us forgiveness and love.
We ask your blessing upon our homes and on all who have guided and helped us.
We pray for homes where there is strife and bitterness, and where relationships are broken down.
We ask your blessing upon all young people and those who have the care of them.
Lord, in you we trust:
hear us as we call to you.

Holy and Strong One, we pray for all who have suffered through the negligence or violence of others.
We pray for all who are troubled in mind or spirit.
We ask your blessing upon all who are ill or suffering in any way. We pray especially for . . .
We give thanks and pray for all carers and home visitors.
Lord, in you we trust:
hear us as we call to you.

Holy and Strong One, as we rejoice in the communion of saints, we pray today for King Charles and all who have died for their faith.

We ask your blessing upon our loved ones departed. We pray today especially for . . .
Merciful Father,
accept these prayers for the sake of your Son, our Saviour, Jesus Christ.
Amen.

The peace

Trust in the Lord and in his love, know that he is your strength and peace.
The peace of the Lord be always with you.
And also with you.

Blessing

Know that God is your strength and shield, a very present help at all times:
and the blessing of God Almighty, the Father, the Son and the Holy Spirit, be upon you and remain with you always.
Amen.

FEBRUARY

3 FEBRUARY

Anskar

Anskar (801–65) was born near Amiens in Picardy. He was educated by his noble family at the nearby Corbie monastery. He became a monk at the age of 13. Later he moved to Corvey in Westphalia (the region between the rivers Rhine and Weser) where he began his work as a missionary. King Harold of Denmark became a Christian while in exile, and he asked Anskar to return with him to evangelise his people. Anskar was consecrated as Bishop of Hamburg in 832 and, after the sack of Hamburg by the Vikings in 845, he was made Archbishop of Hamburg and Bremen by Pope Nicholas I. He founded schools, cared for the poor, and helped in the lessening of the Viking slave trade. He sought to lead the simplest of lives, wearing a hair shirt and only eating bread and drinking water, when his health allowed it. He died at Bremen and was buried there.

Readings

Isaiah 52:7-10
Romans 10:11-15
Mark 1:14-20

Opening prayer

God, who called Anskar to proclaim the Good News among the Nordic people, and to witness to your love and compassion, grant that we might heed your call to tell of your love and show your compassion in our lives: we ask this in love of Jesus, who with you, Father, and the Holy Spirit, are our God now and forever.

Intercessions

God of love, we praise you for Anskar, and pray for the Church in Nordic lands.
We ask your blessing upon all who preach the Word and celebrate the Sacraments, and pray especially for . . .

We remember before you the Church's work among the poor and those in captivity.
We pray for the work and witness of CAFOD, Christian Aid and Amnesty International, and for all who work as prison chaplains.
Lord, hear us,
and keep us in your peace.

God of love, we remember before you areas of the world where people are judged by the colour of their skin, their gender, or their social standing, and where people suffer from prejudice.
We pray for all who are imprisoned through the greed and injustice of others.
We ask forgiveness for our own prejudices and pray we may be more compassionate towards all.
We ask your blessing upon all who work to bring justice, freedom and peace to our world.
Lord, hear us,
and keep us in your peace.

God of love, we ask your blessing upon all who seek to uphold and strengthen family life.
We remember the work of the Mothers' Union.
We pray for all who are helping families in trouble and pray for social workers and Citizens Advice in their work.
We pray for our own family and that we may be more attentive and sensitive to each other.
Lord, hear us,
and keep us in your peace.

God of love, we pray for all who are restricted by any sort of disability or disfigurement.
We pray for all who are in permanent care for their own safety.
We ask your blessing upon all those who work in mental health services and those in their care.
We pray for all who are ill at this time, and in silence pray for friends and loved ones who are ill . . .
Lord, hear us,
and keep us in your peace.

God of love, we give thanks for our redemption and pray for Anskar and all the faithful departed.
We pray for those who have died this week, especially . . . and remember our own loved ones who are departed from us.
Merciful Father,
accept these prayers for the sake of your Son, our Saviour, Jesus Christ.
Amen.

The peace

Come to the Lord and love him with all your heart, abide in his peace and share his peace.
The peace of the Lord be always with you.
And also with you.

Blessing

Know that the Lord in his steadfast love is your strength and refuge, and the blessing of God Almighty, the Father, the Son and the Holy Spirit, be upon you and remain with you always.
Amen.

14 FEBRUARY

Cyril and Methodius

Cyril (826–69) and Methodius (815–85) were brothers born in Thessalonica. Both became priests and went to Constantinople. Here Constantine, the name of Cyril before he became a monk, was made the librarian at Sancta Sophia. Both brothers were gifted in their ability to learn languages. The emperor sent them to be missionaries in Moravia (c.863) at the request of the local ruler, who wanted them to teach in the vernacular. They translated some of the Scriptures and the Liturgy into Slavonic, inventing the alphabet to do it; the Cyrillic alphabet is based on this. Because of this they are regarded as the founders of Slavonic literature. However, other missionaries from Germany opposed them and their Eastern approach to worship and they were forced to leave. Constantine became a monk in Rome and took the name of Cyril, but he died soon after in 869. Methodius was consecrated Bishop of Sirmium and returned to Moravia. Again he faced opposition and was imprisoned for two years. Pope John Paul II nominated them as patrons of Europe along with St Benedict.

Readings

Isaiah 52:7-10
Romans 10:11-15
Luke 9:57-62

Opening prayer

God, who revealed the Good News to the Slavonic people through the brothers Cyril and Methodius and their talent for languages, grant that we may hear and understand your word, and through it be brought to a deeper awareness and love of you: through Jesus Christ, who with you and the Holy Spirit, are one God forever and ever.

Intercessions

God our creator, we give you thanks for Cyril and Methodius, and we ask your blessing upon the Church in Europe and upon all who work for unity.
We pray for all who translate the Scriptures and who communicate the Good News to others.
We remember all who build up your Church through faithfulness in prayer and in service and who encourage others to do the same.
Lord, may we learn to use our talents and abilities in your service.
Lord, your kingdom come,
on earth as it is in heaven.

God our creator, we give you thanks for writers, artists, musicians and craftspeople who work to enrich your world and our lives.
We ask your blessing upon all research workers and scientists.
We remember all who work in conservation and the protection of endangered species.
We pray for all who are helping young people to find their abilities and gifts.
Lord, your kingdom come,
on earth as it is in heaven.

God our creator, we give you thanks for our homes and our loved ones.
We ask your blessing upon all who work to maintain and improve the communities to which we belong.
We pray for where we work and for all local industries and employers.
Lord, may we be aware and welcoming to all who are new to our area.
Lord, your kingdom come,
on earth as it is in heaven.

God our creator, we give you thanks for all who care for the health of the nation in the National Health Service, and pray for your blessing upon all who work with those who are ill.
We pray for all who are distressed or disturbed at this time and for all who cannot cope on their own.
We pray for those who work in a hospice and all who are there at this time.
We remember friends and loved ones who are ill, and in silence pray for those whom we know . . .
Lord, your kingdom come,
on earth as it is in heaven.

God our creator, we give you thanks for the brothers Cyril and Methodius and for all your saints in glory.
We remember those who have died recently or whose memorial it is.
We ask your blessing upon friends and loved ones departed: may they rejoice in the glory of your kingdom.
Merciful Father,
accept these prayers for the sake of your Son, our Saviour, Jesus Christ.
Amen.

The peace

Strong and steadfast is God's love for you, and he seeks to enfold you in his peace.
The peace of the Lord be always with you.
And also with you.

Blessing

God's presence goes with you.
God is all about you.
God gives you his love
and fills you with his peace,
and the blessing of God Almighty, the Father, the Son and the Holy Spirit, be upon you and remain with you always.
Amen.

17 FEBRUARY

Janani Luwum

Janani Luwum (1922–77) was born in Acholi in Uganda. He spent much of his childhood and youth as a goatherd, but showed a great talent for learning and absorbing knowledge. He became a teacher and in 1948 was converted to Christianity. A year later he began to study at Buwalasi Theological College and was ordained in 1956. In 1969 he was consecrated as Bishop of Northern Uganda and Archbishop of Uganda in 1974. Idi Amin had come to power in 1971 through a military coup. His harsh rule and brutality were much criticised by the Church and others. Janani and some bishops sent a letter of protest against the virtual sanctioning of state murder. Soon after this, Archbishop Luwum and two government officers were supposedly killed in a car accident. Their bullet-riddled bodies proved that they had been murdered at the instigation of Amin.

Readings

Ecclesiasticus 4:20-28
Romans 8:35-end
John 12:24-32

Opening prayer

Holy and Strong One, we give thanks for Janani Lulum. Remembering how he bravely spoke out against evil, we ask that we may be brave in our witness for the truth and stand firm in what we believe; we ask this in the name of Christ, who died for us and lives and reigns with you and the Holy Spirit, forever and ever.

Intercessions

God, our strength and shield, we remember that Christians are still suffering for their faith and some are being put to death; we pray for all who are in trouble.

We ask your blessing upon the Church in areas of conflict, danger and where power is misused.
We pray for the Church in Uganda, its Archbishop, bishops and all the faithful.
We ask that the Church may always be seen as strength against evil.
Holy and Strong One,
keep us strong in our faith.

God, our strength and shield, we ask your blessing upon all who work for the freedom and wellbeing of others, especially those who risk their lives.
We pray for areas of conflict and where people are forced off their land and out of their homes.
We pray for all who live in refugee camps, shanty towns or deprived areas.
We pray for all who govern our land and who seek peace and justice.
Holy and Strong One,
keep us strong in our faith.

God, our strength and shield, we pray for families torn apart by war, conflict or disaster.
We pray for all who are seeking a solution to the present refugee crisis and all the homeless people.
We give thanks for all we have, and ask your blessing upon our homes, loved ones and friends.
We pray for members of our families who live in other places and lands.
Holy and Strong One,
keep us strong in our faith.

God, our strength and shield, we remember all families that suffer from tyranny, neglect or injustice.
We pray for all who have loved ones in prison or captivity.
We bring before you all who have suffered from accident or injury this week.
We pray for all who are ill, remembering especially . . . and praying in silence for others known to us.
Holy and Strong One,
keep us strong in our faith.

God, our strength and shield, we give you thanks for the faithful witness of Janani Luwum and ask your blessing upon all the faithful departed.
We remember those whose memorial it is, or those for whom we want to pray . . .
Merciful Father,
accept these prayers for the sake of your Son, our Saviour, Jesus Christ.
Amen.

The peace

The deep peace of the Prince of peace fill your hearts and minds that you may live in his peace and light.
The peace of the Lord be always with you.
And also with you.

Blessing

The God of peace deliver you from all evil,
strengthen you in all goodness,
and keep you in the life which is eternal:
and the blessing of God Almighty, the Father, the Son and the Holy Spirit, be upon you and remain with you always.
Amen.

23 FEBRUARY

Polycarp

Polycarp was the Bishop of Smyrna on the Adriatic coast for over 40 years. Tradition says he knew and was a disciple of the apostle St John. Polycarp was known for his wisdom and for standing against heresies. In a wave of persecutions against Christians, Polycarp was offered his life if he would only renounce Christ. He replied, 'I have been Christ's servant for 86 years and he has done me no harm. How can I blaspheme my King and my Saviour?' He was immediately burnt at the stake. His death was in the year 155.

Readings

Wisdom 4:10-15
Revelation 2:8-11
John 15:18-21

Opening prayer

Father, we give you thanks for Polycarp and all the early saints who gave their lives standing against evil, and ask your blessing upon all who remain faithful to Christ in dangerous and difficult circumstances; we ask this in the name of Jesus our Saviour, who lives and reigns with you and the Holy Spirit, forever and ever.

Intercessions

God of grace and goodness, we ask guidance and protection upon the Church in the Middle East and Asia.
We pray for Christians who are persecuted and in danger.
We pray that the church to which we belong may speak out and act against all evil.
We ask your blessing upon our bishop, the clergy and all who profess the faith in our area.
God of love,
make us aware of your presence.

God of grace and goodness, we pray for all who maintain justice and peace.
We remember all who are seeking to bring a fair deal for all, and we pray for Fair Trade.
We pray that none may be overcome by greed or a wrong sense of power.
We ask your blessing upon the United Nations and all who work for peace.
God of love,
make us aware of your presence.

God of grace and goodness, we give thanks for all who have enriched our surroundings by their own efforts and we ask your blessing upon them.
We pray for our own homes and loved ones, and that we all may know your love.
We ask your guidance upon all who help families in distress or trouble.
We pray for all carers and home visitors and all who seek to bring joy and peace to others.
God of love,
make us aware of your presence.

God of grace and goodness, we remember all who struggle with doubt or despair, all who walk in darkness.
We pray for all whose lives are disturbed by past events.
We ask your blessing upon those who seek to support them and relieve their suffering.
We remember all who are ill at this time and pray especially for . . .
God of love,
make us aware of your presence.

God of grace and goodness, we give thanks that, in your love and mercy, life is eternal. We pray for Polycarp and all martyrs, and we remember before you our loved ones departed . . .
Merciful Father,
accept these prayers for the sake of your Son, our Saviour, Jesus Christ. Amen.

The peace

God give you grace to follow his saints, deliver you from all evil and fill your life with his peace.
The peace of the Lord be always with you.
And also with you.

Blessing

The Lord of life strengthen and guide you throughout this day and always:
and the blessing of God Almighty, the Father, the Son and the Holy Spirit, be upon you and remain with you always.
Amen.

27 FEBRUARY

George Herbert

George Herbert (1593–1633) was born into an aristocratic family in Pembroke in Wales. He was educated at Westminster School and Trinity College, Cambridge. He eventually became Public Orator in the University and then a Member of Parliament. It looked as if he was to have a future career at court. To everyone's surprise, he felt called to be ordained. After spending some time with his friend Nicholas Ferrar at Little Gidding, he was made deacon in 1626, and then married in 1629. The following year he was priested and offered the living of Bemerton, near Salisbury. He was known for excellent pastoral care. He was a prolific writer of hymns and a poet. He wrote the treatise *The Country Parson* on the life of a priest. Among his best-loved hymns is 'Teach me, my God and King, in all things thee to see'.

Readings

Malachi 2:5-7
Revelation 19:5-9
Matthew 11:25-end

Opening prayer

Gracious God, we give you thanks that you called George Herbert to be a pastor of your people and a leader in worship, and ask you by your grace and goodness to guide us into ways that reveal that you are the King of Glory and the King of Peace: we ask this in the name of Jesus Christ our Lord.

Intercessions

King of Glory, we give thanks for the writings, hymns and example of George Herbert.
We ask your blessing upon all poets and hymn writers, upon all who lead and write prayers.

We pray for the pastoral work of the Church and ask your blessing upon all who do this work.
May your Church be known for its care in the community.
King of Glory, hear us.
King of Peace, help us.

King of Glory, we ask your blessing upon all leaders and rulers of people and upon our government.
We remember those who suffer under tyrants and despots, and we pray for all whose lives are endangered by speaking out.
We pray for all who care for flocks, herdsmen and shepherds.
We ask your blessing upon all who work to protect animals and care for the preservation of flora and fauna.
King of Glory, hear us.
King of Peace, help us.

King of Glory, we ask your blessing upon all who enrich our homes through music, art and crafts.
We remember all who provide for our daily needs.
We ask your blessing upon our loved ones and friends: may our love reflect your love.
We remember all who are lonely within our community and pray that we may show pastoral care.
King of Glory, hear us.
King of Peace, help us.

King of Glory, we pray for all who are not at peace with themselves, their neighbours or with you.
We remember communities that are divided by old rivalries, prejudice or fear.
We pray for all who are suffering at this time.
We remember, in a moment of silence, those we know who are ill.
King of Glory, hear us.
King of Peace, help us.

King of Glory, we thank you for all who have served you faithfully and are in your kingdom of peace.
We remember those who have died recently . . .

In a moment of silence, we pray for our loved ones departed . . .
Merciful Father,
accept these prayers for the sake of your Son, our Saviour, Jesus Christ.
Amen.

The peace

Abide in him, who is the King of Glory,
and he will share with you his light and his peace.
The peace of the Lord be always with you.
And also with you.

Blessing

God, of grace and glory, grant you his guidance and lead you into his peace and his love: and the blessing of God Almighty, the Father, the Son and the Holy Spirit, be upon you and remain with you always.
Amen.

MARCH

2 MARCH

Chad

Chad was the youngest of four brothers; all became priests and two were bishops. They all went to Lindisfarne to be educated as part of Aidan's first pupils. Later Chad was sent to Ireland to continue his education. He returned to Lastingham in North Yorkshire, where his brother Cedd had founded a monastery. He returned at the request of Cedd, who was ill with the plague, as was their brother Cynebil. The year was 664; Chad arrived in the November to find that both his brothers were dead and buried. Chad continued to be in charge of Lastingham as its abbot. Wilfrid, who had been appointed Bishop of York, had not returned from the continent, so Chad was chosen as the bishop in the year 666. It was still the time of the plague and there was hardly a bishop to be found in England. The Archbishop of Canterbury was dead and so was his appointed successor. The Bishop of Rochester was dying. To be consecrated, Chad had to go to Wini of Dorchester and he was assisted by two British – that is, Celtic – bishops. Chad returned to Lastingham from where he did his work as the Bishop of York. Wilfrid returned but went to the monastery at Ripon. In 669 Theodore, the new Archbishop of Canterbury, removed Chad from the post and gave it to Wilfrid, as he had been appointed to it. Chad was soon after made the Bishop of Mercia; he had a monastery at Lichfield built from where he would work, and another at Barrow in Lincolnshire. Chad was known to be devout and humble and a missionary bishop. He died on this day in 672.

Readings

Isaiah 6:1-8
1 Timothy 2:11b-16
Matthew 24:42-46

Opening prayer

God, we give thanks that you called Chad and his three brothers to a life of dedication and holiness. As Chad walked among his people as a pastor and evangelist, may we walk gently upon the earth and show our respect for all we meet: we ask this in the name of him who walked among us, Jesus Christ our Lord.

Intercessions

Holy Lord, we give thanks for the training of Chad and his brothers on Lindisfarne, and we ask your blessing upon all who are training for the ministry.
We ask your blessing upon the churches of Lindisfarne and Lastingham, and pray for the dioceses of York and of Lichfield.
We ask your blessing upon our bishop and the clergy of our area.
May your Church be known for its outreach and care for the world.
Holy and Mighty God,
hear us and help us.

Holy Lord, we ask your blessing upon all who seek to care for the world's climate, its oceans and its diversity of life.
We pray for all who are involved in the management of land and the right use of resources.
We ask your guidance upon all in power who make decisions concerning the future of the world and our wellbeing.
We remember the world's poor and oppressed people and all involved in their care.
Holy and Mighty God,
hear us and help us.

Holy Lord, we ask your blessing upon all who have the care of young people.
We pray for nurseries, play schools, schools and colleges.
We remember our local organisations for young people and their leaders.
We pray for all children separated from their parents, especially those taken into care and in need of protection.
We give thanks and pray for our own homes and loved ones.
Holy and Mighty God,
hear us and help us.

Holy Lord, we remember all who have been involved in natural disasters, especially . . .
We pray for all who feel they are caught up in the storms of life.
We ask your blessing upon all who are ill at home or in hospital, and in silence pray for those whom we know.
We pray for all who are terminally ill and for those caring for them.
Holy and Mighty God,
hear us and help us.

Holy Lord, we give thanks for St Chad and all who have built up your Church.
We pray for Chad and, in silence, all our loved ones departed . . .
Merciful Father,
accept these prayers for the sake of your Son, our Saviour, Jesus Christ. Amen.

The peace

God is your strength and your salvation; he is your peace and in him is the fullness of life.
The peace of the Lord be always with you.
And also with you.

Blessing

God be with you now and forever.
God be your strength.
God be your peace:
and the blessing of God Almighty, the Father, the Son and the Holy Spirit, be upon you and remain with you always.
Amen.

7 MARCH

Perpetua, Felicity and her companions

Vibia Perpetua was a young married noblewoman of Carthage who had given birth to a son a few months before she was arrested under the persecution of Septimus Severus. He had forbidden any fresh conversions to Christianity. Perpetua and her pregnant slave, Felicity, were among a group of catechumens. Revocatus was Felicity's husband, and with Saturnius and Secundus, was also among those martyred for their faith. The contemporary account concentrates on the women. Perpetua and her child were imprisoned, and Felicity gave birth in prison. It was reported that these young women left prison joyfully, as if they were on their way to heaven. Perpetua sang a hymn of praise to God. The women were put into the arena with a mad heifer. After this, when the gladiators were to put them to death, Perpetua guided the trembling gladiator's knife to her throat.

Readings

Wisdom 3:1-7
Revelation 12:10-12a
Matthew 10:34-39

Opening prayer

God, our Saviour, we give you thanks for the saints and martyrs of Africa, remembering especially today St Perpetua and her companions: as they were given strength to stand firm in their faith, guide us and keep us faithful to you and lead us into the ways of peace: we ask this in the love of Christ our Saviour.

Intercessions

Ever loving God, we remember all who are faithful to you amid persecution and the risk of their lives.
We ask your blessing upon those who have lost their work or their homes because of their faith.
We give thanks for all who dedicate their lives to teach us the faith and to lead us in worship; we pray especially for . . .
We pray for the Church in Africa and its witness to your love and the power of the resurrection.
Saving God,
hear us and help us.

Ever loving God, we ask your blessing upon all who guide and direct our young folk and help them to live full lives.
We pray for all support agencies in their care for people in need or in difficulties.
We remember all who have enriched our country and community by their generosity and talent, and we pray especially for . . .
May we find areas where we can be useful and generous in our giving.
Saving God,
hear us and help us.

Ever loving God, we ask your blessing upon our homes and all our loved ones.
We remember homes where there is poverty and those who are homeless.
We pray for all who live among fear and violence and whose lives or wellbeing are endangered.
We give thanks for all who teach our hearts to sing and to rejoice in life.
Saving God,
hear us and help us.

Ever loving God, we remember all who are permanently suffering, in pain or distress.
We pray for all who have suffered through accidents or disasters.
We ask your blessing upon friends and loved ones who are ill,
(in silence let us pray for those we know).

We pray for all who have been recently bereaved.
Saving God,
hear us and help us.

Ever loving God, as we rejoice in the witness of Perpetua and her companions, we give you thanks for eternal life.
We pray for the faithful departed, remembering especially today . . .
Merciful Father,
accept these prayers for the sake of your Son, our Saviour, Jesus Christ. Amen.

The peace

The peace of the Creator give you strength.
The peace of the Saviour warm your heart.
The peace of the Spirit bring you rest.
The peace of the Lord be always with you.
And also with you.

Blessing

God, in his power, protect you from all evil, enfold you in his peace and keep you in life eternal: and the blessing of God Almighty, the Father, the Son and the Holy Spirit, be upon you and remain with you always. **Amen.**

8 MARCH

Edward King, Bishop of Lincoln

Edward King (1829–1910) was born in London. After being ordained, he became chaplain and then the Principal of Cuddesdon Theological College and Professor of Theology at Oxford. In both these places he influenced many who were training for the priesthood. In 1885 he was made Bishop of Lincoln. He was a good pastoral bishop and attended to the needs of many, both clergy and laity. He was widely respected for his wisdom and personal holiness, though his Catholic principles and theology were often cause for controversy.

Readings

Malachi 2:5-7
Hebrews 13:1-8
Matthew 23:8-12

Opening prayer

Heavenly Father, we give you thanks and praise for the work and life of Edward King, for his teaching, pastoral care and personal witness to your love. May we reveal your love and compassion in our lives and draw others to know and love you: we ask this in the name of Christ our Lord.

Intercessions

God of grace and goodness, we give thanks for all who have been faithful shepherds of those entrusted into their care.
We pray today for the diocese of Lincoln, its bishop and people.
We pray for our bishop . . . and our vicar or minister . . .
We ask your blessing upon all who seek out the lost to give them help and compassion.
Loving Lord, hear us
and help us.

God of grace and goodness, we pray for all who care for sheep, goats or cattle and are their shepherds and herdsmen and women.
We remember all who have the responsibility of caring for animals of any sort.
We pray for vets and for the work of the RSPCA.
We pray for world leaders and their care of their people.
We remember Elizabeth our Queen and our government.
Loving Lord, hear us
and help us.

God of grace and goodness, we give thanks for all who show hospitality to others and ask your blessing upon their care.
May our homes be places of welcome, compassion, care and peace.
We ask your blessing upon all who feel lost or unwanted.
We pray for all social events in our area, in clubs, pubs and local organisations.
Loving Lord, hear us
and help us.

God of grace and goodness, we remember all who are in need of friendship, help or care.
We pray for the housebound and those who are lonely.
We pray for families where a parent is away from home or in prison.
We ask your blessing upon all who are ill at home or in hospital; we remember especially . . .
Loving Lord, hear us
and help us.

God of grace and goodness, we give thanks for Edward King and all who have been our pastoral helpers and are now departed from us.
We ask your blessing upon all who have died recently, especially . . .
(and in a moment of silence) we pray for our loved ones departed.
Merciful Father,
accept these prayers for the sake of your Son, our Saviour, Jesus Christ. Amen.

The peace

The peace of God be in your heart and mind,
in your actions and in your words,
that you may share his peace wherever you go.
The peace of the Lord be always with you.
And also with you.

Blessing

God look upon you with his deep compassion, surround you with his love,
guide you in all difficulties,
keep you in life eternal:
and the blessing of God Almighty, the Father, the Son and the Holy Spirit, be upon you and remain with you always.
Amen.

20 MARCH

Cuthbert

Cuthbert was born of well-off parents in Northumbria. At an early age he was known to be a man of prayer. The night that St Aidan died, Cuthbert, up in the hills guarding sheep, had a vision of a holy soul rising up to heaven. When he was told Aidan had died, he decided to dedicate his own life to the service of God, and sought to join the monks at Melrose Abbey. Whilst there, he was made the Prior. He also made many pastoral visits to the poor and into the hill country. After the Synod of Whitby in 664 he became the Prior of Lindisfarne, with Eata from Melrose as the Bishop. This was to help the Celtic monastery of Lindisfarne to adopt the Catholic traditions and dating of Easter. After 12 years he sought release from his post to become a hermit on the island of Inner Farne. It was from there he was called to be a bishop in 685. His pastoral care was shown in his visiting all over his large diocese, in preaching, teaching, consecrating churches and healing people. Into his third year as bishop, he asked to be relieved from his duties to return to Inner Farne for the last months of his life, and he died there in 687.

Readings

Ezekiel 34:11-13, 15
1 Corinthians 5:14-20
Matthew 18:12-14

Opening prayer

God our creator, who called Cuthbert to proclaim the gospel, open our ears to your call to us, that we also may show the Good News in our lives and witness to your presence among us: through Christ Jesus our Lord.

Intercessions

Lord of life, we give thanks for the life and witness of St Cuthbert, and for the heritage of the Lindisfarne Gospels.
We ask your blessing upon the Church on Lindisfarne, at Melrose and the Cathedral of Durham.
We pray for all who preach and minister the sacraments, and for those involved in pastoral care.
May our eyes be opened to your presence and may we walk humbly upon the earth.
Ever present and loving God,
hear us and help us.

Lord of life, we ask your blessing upon all leaders of nations and communities.
We remember Elizabeth our Queen, and our government at local and national levels.
We ask your blessing upon remote communities that are threatened by war or commercial greed.
We pray for areas of poverty, plague or natural disasters, remembering especially at this time . . .
We ask that you will strengthen and guide all who work for justice, peace and freedom.
Ever present and loving God,
hear us and help us.

Lord of life, we give thanks for all who uphold and rejoice in family life.
We pray for homes where there is a new member within the family, and for children recently adopted or taken into care.
We ask your blessing upon families where someone is ill or distressed.
We pray for any families where there is tension or violence.
Ever present and loving God,
hear us and help us.

Lord of life, we ask your blessing upon any who suffer from leprosy or a disfigurement in their lives.
We pray for those who are in constant pain or are terminally ill.
Lord, be a strength to all who care for the suffering peoples of our world.
We ask your blessing upon friends and loved ones who are ill, especially . . .
Ever present and loving God,
hear us and help us.

Lord of life, we give thanks for St Cuthbert and that life in you is eternal. We pray for all the saints in glory and ask your blessing upon our friends and loved ones departed from us. (In silence let us pray for those whom we want to remember.)
Merciful Father,
accept these prayers for the sake of your Son, our Saviour, Jesus Christ. Amen.

The peace

Christ, the Good Shepherd, go with you
to protect you,
to shelter you,
to keep you in his peace.
The peace of the Lord be always with you.
And also with you.

Blessing

Go out in peace with the love of God in your heart,
the light of God in your eyes,
the goodness of God on your lips:
and the blessing of God Almighty, the Father, the Son and the Holy Spirit, be upon you and remain with you always.
Amen.

21 MARCH

Thomas Cranmer

Thomas Cranmer was born at Aslockton in Nottinghamshire in 1489. After studying at Cambridge he joined the diplomatic service in 1527. He helped Henry VIII in seeking the annulment of his marriage to Catherine of Aragon. He was made Archbishop of Canterbury in 1533 and duly pronounced the marriage of Catherine of Aragon null and void. He worked closely with Thomas Cromwell and was responsible for producing the Book of Common Prayer in 1549 and 1552. The quality of Cranmer's prose left a standard for the Church of England. Under the reign of Queen Mary, he was convicted of treason in 1553 and heresy in 1554. He signed recantations but was still condemned to be burnt at the stake in 1556; he made a last strong affirmation of his Protestant faith before he was burnt to death.

Readings

Isaiah 43:1-7
2 Timothy 2:3-7 (8-13)
John 10:11-16

Opening prayer

Gracious God, we give you thanks for Archbishop Thomas Cranmer, for his work to provide the Church with a prayer book, for his sense of poetry and his good use of the English language. May we be faithful in our prayers and in our worship and rejoice before you each day: we ask this in the name of Christ our Lord.

Intercessions

God our Creator, we give thanks for Archbishop Cranmer and the Book of Common Prayer.
We pray for the Archbishop of Canterbury and for the worldwide Anglican Communion.

We ask your guidance upon the Church in times of difficult decisions which challenge its unity.
We pray for all who work to provide people with prayers in their own language.
Lord, hear our prayers
and be our strength and shield.

God our Creator, we ask your blessing upon all who teach our language and give us a sense of its beauty and poetry.
We pray for all who seek to express the deep things of life in poetry and literature, music and art.
We pray for all who teach in schools, colleges and universities and remember today our local schools and education services.
We remember all who have learning difficulties and those with impaired vision or hearing.
Lord, hear our prayers
and be our strength and shield.

God our Creator, we pray for all who do not get the opportunity of a good education.
We ask your blessing upon the children in our local schools.
We give thanks for all who provide us with means of relaxation and recreation within our community.
We pray for our homes, our loved ones and our friends.
Lord, hear our prayers
and be our strength and shield.

God our Creator, we pray for areas where freedom of speech is denied.
We remember areas where people are under harsh rule and oppressive regimes.
We pray for all who are suffering, in sorrow, or in danger.
We ask your blessing upon all who are ill (and in a moment of silence we offer our prayers for any known to us).
Lord, hear our prayers
and be our strength and shield.

God our Creator, we give thanks for Thomas Cranmer, for his witness and faith.
We pray for all the faithful departed, especially any who are dear to us.
Lord, may we all be numbered with your saints in glory everlasting.
Merciful Father,
accept these prayers for the sake of your Son, our Saviour, Jesus Christ.
Amen.

The peace

Rejoice in the Lord,
in his presence,
in his power,
and in his peace.
The peace of the Lord be always with you.
And also with you.

Blessing

May the light of the gospel shine in your lives,
the love of the Lord be in your hearts,
the peace of God in all your dealings:
and the blessing of God Almighty, the Father, the Son and the Holy Spirit, be upon you and remain with you always.
Amen.

APRIL

10 APRIL

William Law

William Law was born at Kings Cliffe in Northamptonshire in 1686. He was educated at Emmanuel College, Cambridge. He became a Fellow of the College in 1711 after he had been ordained deacon. When George I came to the throne, William refused to take the Oath of Allegiance, because he believed that the deposed James II was the true king and his heirs should occupy the throne. He lost his fellowship but in 1728 he was made priest. This was the same year that he published *A Serious Call to the Devout Life*, which had a strong influence on John and Charles Wesley, and also upon Samuel Johnson. He returned to Kings Cliffe in 1740 where he led a life of prayer, simplicity and caring for the poor. He died there on this day in 1761.

Readings

1 Kings 3:(6-10), 11-14
1 Corinthians 2:9 to end
Matthew 17:1-9

Opening prayer

God, who called William Law to serve you faithfully as he sought to live a devout and holy life of pastoral care and looking after the poor, strengthen us to follow his example of prayer and compassion that we may serve you all our days: we ask this in the power of Christ our Lord.

Intercessions

Holy God, as we give thanks for William Law who served you in a devout and holy life, may we seek to work for you in love and peace.
We pray for all members of the worldwide Church that they may be faithful to their calling.

We ask your blessing upon all who are called to minister to others and those who serve you through the ordained ministry.
We pray for all who write books on the faith and who teach people to pray.
We pray for our parish church and for its ministry to the community.
God, as you have called us,
make us worthy of our calling.

Holy God, we pray for those helping young people to find their way in life and to fulfil themselves in their work.
We ask your blessing upon all who work to keep peace in our world, and we pray for the work of the United Nations.
We pray for leaders of people and nations; we ask your blessing upon Elizabeth our Queen and all in authority under her.
We pray that all who are called to high office may remember they are called to serve.
God, as you have called us,
make us worthy of our calling.

Holy God, we thank you for all who helped us to find our way in life and to develop our talents and abilities.
We pray for all who teach, and ask your blessing upon our local schools, nurseries and play schools.
We give thanks for all who quietly come to the aid of others in caring and compassion.
We pray for our homes and our loved ones, and thank you for all they have brought to our lives.
God, as you have called us,
make us worthy of our calling.

Holy God, we give thanks for our freedom, and pray for all who have lost work or homes through prejudice, illness or oppression.
We remember the countless homeless people of our world, the street children and the refugees.
We ask your blessing upon all who are called to relieve pain, sorrow or anxiety.
We remember all ill people and pray especially for those known to us . . .
God, as you have called us,
make us worthy of our calling.

Holy God, we give thanks for William Law and all who have sought to lead a holy and devout life.
(In a moment of silence) we pray for all those whom we love and are departed from us, that they may rejoice in the fullness of life eternal.
Merciful Father,
accept these prayers for the sake of your Son, our Saviour, Jesus Christ.
Amen.

The peace

Go out in the love of God,
with his grace to guide you,
and his peace within you.
The peace of the Lord be always with you.
And also with you.

Blessing

Love the Lord your God,
with all your heart,
with all your mind,
with all your strength:
and the blessing of God Almighty, the Father, the Son and the Holy Spirit, be upon you and remain with you always.
Amen.

19 APRIL

Alphege

Alphege was a monk at Deerhurst near Gloucester but later withdrew to become a hermit in Somerset. St Dunstan, when Archbishop of Canterbury, called him back to be Abbot of Bath, then in 984 he became the Bishop of Winchester. After this he became the Archbishop of Canterbury in 1005. He continued to live a simple lifestyle and was lavish in his giving of alms to the poor. He was much loved and respected. In 1011 the Danes overran all of south-east England, Canterbury was sacked, the cathedral burned and Alphege held for the ransom of £3000 which was an enormous amount. Alphege forbade anyone to pay it, knowing it would impoverish so many people. Nine months later, the Danes finally killed him by pelting him with ox bones and dispatching him with the blow of an axe at Greenwich in 1012.

Readings

Isaiah 43:1-7
Hebrews 5:1-4
Matthew 16:24-26

Opening prayer

Holy God, Holy and Strong One, we give you thanks for the courage and self-sacrifice of Alphege when he was the Archbishop of Canterbury: may we have the courage to stand against oppression and show our compassion for all who are oppressed: we ask this in the name of our Saviour, Christ our Lord.

Intercessions

Generous God, we give you praise for the love and sacrifice shown in the life of Alphege.
Lord, as he was generous towards the poor, teach us to be generous in our dealings.

We ask your blessing upon the dioceses of Canterbury and Winchester and all who live within them.
We pray for all who teach of your love and draw others to know your presence.
God of grace and goodness,
be our strength and shield.

Generous God, we ask your guidance upon all world leaders, that we may be brought to peace and justice in our world.
May the ears and the hearts of all be open to the cry of the poor and distressed.
We pray for all who care for the earth and the diversity of life upon it.
We give thanks for all who stand up for oppressed peoples and who work for their freedom and safety.
God of grace and goodness,
be our strength and shield.

Generous God, teach us to be sensitive and caring towards all we meet.
Where possible, may we be of help with the needs of family and friends, and have the humility to accept their help.
We pray for homes where there is lack of love or proper care for each other.
We ask your blessing of peace upon us, our homes and our community.
God of grace and goodness,
be our strength and shield.

Generous God, we remember before you all who are held as prisoners through tyranny and injustice.
We pray for any whose lives are endangered by the violence and greed of others.
We pray for the world's poor who feel they are forgotten or rejected by those with plenty.
We pray for all who are ill (and in a moment of silence, pray for any we know of) . . .
God of grace and goodness,
be our strength and shield.

Generous God, we give thanks for all who have given their lives that others might live in peace and in freedom and today we remember Alphege.

We pray for all who have died recently, especially . . . (and in a moment of stillness, we pray for all our loved ones departed, that they may rejoice in glory).
Merciful Father,
accept these prayers for the sake of your Son, our Saviour, Jesus Christ.
Amen.

The peace

The God of peace fill you with all joy and peace as you put your trust in him.
The peace of the Lord be always with you.
And also with you.

Blessing

The presence of God our Father,
the peace of Christ our Saviour,
the power of the Holy Spirit be with you:
and the blessing of God Almighty, the Father, the Son and the Holy Spirit, be upon you and remain with you always.
Amen.

21 APRIL

Anselm

Anselm was born of a rich Lombard family in Italy c.1033. When he was 15 he wanted to become a monk, but his father refused to give his consent. After his mother died, his father made his life difficult so he left home. Attracted by the reputation of Lanfranc, he journeyed to the Benedictine monastery of Bec where Lanfranc was the abbot. He became a monk there and later, in 1078, he became the abbot. As Abbot, Anselm visited England and won the hearts of many people. When Lanfranc, who was now Archbishop of Canterbury, died, Anselm was consecrated as his successor in 1093. However, he faced opposition from the king over issues about the papacy and had to go into exile in 1097. With the accession of Henry I, he returned to England in 1100; but again in quarrels with the king he went into exile again in 1103. After Pope Pascal I advised Anselm to be more moderate in his stance, peace was made and Anselm returned to England after more than three years in exile. He spent the rest of his life in England, showing great care for all in his charge. He died at nearly 80 in 1109.

Readings

Wisdom 9:13-end
Romans 5:8-11
Matthew 24:42-46

Opening prayer

Gracious God, we give thanks for the life and worship of St Anselm and pray:
give us, O Lord, eyes to behold you,
a heart to love you,
a life to proclaim you
in the power of the Spirit
and in the name of Christ our Lord.

Intercessions

We bring before you, O Lord, all who seek to proclaim your love and saving presence.
We remember all who serve in monasteries and convents and who maintain a pattern of daily prayer.
We give thanks for the abbey of Bec and pray for the work of the Bendictines.
We ask your blessing upon the Archbishops of Canterbury and York and all clergy.
Loving and merciful God,
hear us, and help us.

We bring before you, O Lord, the troubles of people and nations,
the fear and needs of the refugees,
the hopelessness of the starving,
places where people seeking sanctuary only find antagonism.
We pray for all relief agencies and for Amnesty International.
Loving and merciful God,
hear us, and help us.

We bring before you, O Lord, all those who are dear to us,
our families and our friends,
those who have taught us and been a support to us,
and we ask your blessing upon them and the schools in our area.
Loving and merciful God,
hear us, and help us.

We bring before you, O Lord, all who are ill,
the weak and the weary,
those needing care at home or in hospital,
all who have suffered from accident or violence.
We remember, in silence, loved ones who are in need.
Loving and merciful God,
hear us, and help us.

We bring before you, O Lord, the anguish of the bereaved,
all who have died this week, especially . . .
and in the stillness we remember friends and loved ones departed,
may they rest in peace and rejoice in your kingdom.
Merciful Father,
accept these prayers for the sake of your Son, our Saviour, Jesus Christ.
Amen.

The peace

Look upon the world with God's compassion,
speak to all you meet in the love of God,
go on your journey in the peace of God.
The peace of the Lord be always with you.
And also with you.

Blessing

The Lord make his love known to you,
keep you as the apple of his eye,
protect you from all evil,
keep you in life eternal:
and the blessing of God Almighty, the Father, the Son and the Holy Spirit, be upon you and remain with you always.
Amen.

29 APRIL

Catherine of Siena

Catherine was born the youngest of 20 or more children c.1347. Her father was a dyer in the city of Siena. At an early age she was devoted to a life of prayer, in spite of parental opposition. She refused to be married and became a Dominican tertiary. After years of silence and solitude, she began her work of nursing the sick. Though she never learnt to write, through the help of others she dictated her large correspondence. In the last five years of her life, she became involved in the affairs of Church and state. She was invited by Pope Urban VI to Rome to assist him in seeking to heal the schism within the Church. She soon wore herself out working for this cause and died in 1380.

Readings

Proverbs 8:1, 16-21
3 John: 2-8
John 17:12-end

Opening prayer

Saving God, we give you thanks for Catherine of Siena, her devotion to the Passion of Christ, her care of the poor, and her work as an advisor in the need to keep unity within the Church. May we seek to serve Christ in the needy and reveal your saving power in our lives: we ask this in the name of Christ our Saviour.

Intercessions

Lord of our salvation, we give you praise for the life and witness of St Catherine of Siena.
We ask your blessing upon all religious communities, retreat houses and places of prayer.

We pray for the work of the Church in areas of oppression and poverty.
May we in our lives reveal your love and your saving grace.
Saving God,
be our strength and our shield.

Lord of our salvation, we pray for all ambassadors of peace and for those who seek to maintain unity in our world.
We ask your blessing upon those who seek to protect the unique identity and diversity of nations and peoples.
We remember the work of the United Nations and peace-keeping forces.
We pray for peoples and nations that are divided through prejudice or hatred.
Saving God,
be our strength and our shield.

Lord of our salvation, we ask that we may be at home with you in our homes and live in love and joy.
We remember families that are going through a difficult time and are finding it hard to cope.
We remember those who are separated from their loved ones through work or any other reason.
May we share in the life of our community and with those around us.
Saving God,
be our strength and our shield.

Lord of our salvation, we give thanks for all who care for the poor, the ill or the lonely, and ask your blessing upon them.
We pray for doctors, nurses, hospitals and hospices and all care homes.
We remember all who are anxious about their health or that of a loved one.
We pray for friends and loved ones who are ill (as we keep a moment of silence).
Saving God,
be our strength and our shield.

Lord of our salvation, we give thanks for St Catherine and all your saints in glory.
We remember all who have died this week, and pray especially for . . .

We ask your blessing upon our loved ones departed . . .
Merciful Father,
accept these prayers for the sake of your Son, our Saviour, Jesus Christ.
Amen.

The peace

The saving God is with you, to keep you from harm and to give you his peace.
The peace of the Lord be always with you.
And also with you.

Blessing

God be with you to protect you.
God be within you to strengthen you.
God be before you to guide you.
God enfold you in his love:
and the blessing of God Almighty, the Father, the Son and the Holy Spirit, be upon you and remain with you always.
Amen.

MAY

2 MAY

Athanasius

Athanasius (c.296–373) was educated at the Catechetical School in Alexandria and was made deacon under Bishop Alexander. With the bishop he attended and contributed to the Council of Nicaea in 325, where Arianism, which denied the divinity of Christ, was condemned. Athanasius spent the rest of his life defending the orthodox beliefs of the Church. In 328 he succeeded Bishop Alexander as Bishop of Alexandria. Because of his strong stance against Arianism, he was driven into exile more than once. He continued to write while in exile. He wrote on the Incarnation and Redemption, and also wrote on the Scriptures, especially the Psalms. He encouraged monasticism which was in its early stages, and wrote a Life of St Antony. He died on this day in 373.

Readings

Ecclesiasticus 4:20-28
2 Timothy 4:6-8
Matthew 10:24-27

Opening prayer

God our Father, who called Athanasius to be a defender of the divinity of Christ against those who denied it, grant that we may rejoice in your saving love for us and stand firm in our faith: we ask this in the name of Christ our Saviour.

Intercessions

Holy God, as we give you thanks and praise for the life and witness of Athanasius, we pray for the Church in Egypt, especially those who are being persecuted for their faith.
We ask your blessing upon all who stand against false teaching, and seek to lead us into the ways of truth.

We pray for all who teach Religious Education, and all theological colleges.
We ask your blessing upon all training for ministry and upon those recently ordained.
Lord, in your love,
guide us by your light.

Holy God, as we pray for defenders of the faith, we pray for Elizabeth our Queen, and for all in authority under her.
We ask your blessing upon all who work in the media and who influence the minds of others by what they produce.
We pray for the press and those who provide us with daily news, that it will be done with integrity and without bias.
We remember all who champion the poor of our world and seek their wellbeing.
Lord, in your love,
guide us by your light.

Holy God, we ask your blessing upon our homes and loved ones.
We pray for our local community and our schools.
We ask your blessing upon all who work for unity and peace within our area.
We pray for any areas of division, enmity or prejudice, that they may find healing.
Lord, in your love,
guide us by your light.

Holy God, we pray for all who are struggling at this time, that they may know your love and saving power.
We pray for those who have suffered from acts of evil and have lost faith in themselves, others or you.
We pray for all who work in the emergency services and those who risk their lives for others.
We ask your blessing upon all who are ill; (in silence we remember those we know).
Lord, in your love,
guide us by your light.

Holy God, we remember all who are bereaved and in deep grief.
We pray for loved ones left behind and who are fearful of not being able to cope.
We pray for those who have died this week and for loved ones departed who are dear to us . . .
Merciful Father,
accept these prayers for the sake of your Son, our Saviour, Jesus Christ.
Amen.

The peace

The peace of Christ be on your lips.
The peace of Christ be in your heart.
The peace of Christ be in all your dealings.
The peace of the Lord be always with you.
And also with you.

Blessing

God give you grace to stand firm in the faith,
to confess Jesus Christ as your Saviour,
to be guided by his Holy Spirit:
and the blessing of God Almighty, the Father, the Son and the Holy Spirit, be upon you and remain with you always.
Amen.

4 MAY

English Saints and Martyrs of the Reformation

We remember all who witnessed to their faith during the upheavals of the Reformation in England from the fourteenth to the seventeenth century. Many men and women suffered for their faith, not only the Roman Catholics and those of the newly formed Church of England, but many others who sought to stand for what they saw as the truth. We remember those who died for their faith and all who suffered in any way.

Readings

Isaiah 43:1-7
2 Corinthians 4:5-12
John 12:20-26

Opening prayer

Lord God, we join with the saints in glory to give you thanks and praise. We give thanks for the saints of this land, who spread the faith and were a witness of your love. May we, with them, rejoice in your presence and in your saving power: we ask this in the love of Christ, our Lord.

Intercessions

Holy and mighty God, give us grace to be inspired by the saints of this land and to walk in their ways.
Forgive us, Lord, for the prejudice and rigidity that divides the Church and help us to see we are one in you and your love.
May we as your people move towards a greater unity in our service of others and in giving you glory.

We remember all who are being persecuted for their faith, or treated with scorn.
Lord, make us to be numbered with your saints,
in your eternal glory.

Holy and mighty God, we pray for your world, for a deeper unity and peace among all peoples.
Help us to rejoice in the diversity of peoples and traditions and to learn from one another.
Grant us a vision to see we are all one creation, brought forth out of your love.
We ask your blessing upon all who are suffering from war, hunger or oppression.
Lord, make us to be numbered with your saints,
in your eternal glory.

Holy and mighty God, we give you praise for all who have inspired us by their lives, those who have taught us of your presence and revealed your love.
We remember all who have sacrificed for us and were generous with their time and gifts.
We ask your blessing upon our homes that they may be places of love and peace.
May we live generously and be a guide and example to others.
Lord, make us to be numbered with your saints,
in your eternal glory.

Holy and mighty God, we give thanks for all who serve you in the way they work for the care of others.
We pray for those who work among the poor and rejected peoples of our world.
We remember all who help others in emergencies or disasters.
We pray for all who help in the healing of people and nations, and in a moment of silence we pray for any who are ill and known to us . . .
Lord, make us to be numbered with your saints,
in your eternal glory.

Holy and mighty God, we give thanks and praise for the saints of this land and the rich heritage they have left for us.

May we share with them in the glory of your kingdom and help to reveal it here on earth.
We pray for all the departed; we remember those who have died this week . . . (and in silence pray for our own loved ones departed).
Merciful Father,
accept these prayers for the sake of your Son, our Saviour, Jesus Christ.
Amen.

The peace

The Lord has called you by your name
to reveal in your life his love and his peace.
The peace of the Lord be always with you.
And also with you.

Blessing

God give you grace to grow in the faith,
to resist evil, to work for the good of all:
and the blessing of God Almighty, the Father, the Son and the Holy Spirit, be upon you and remain with you always.
Amen.

8 MAY

Julian of Norwich

Julian was born in 1342. In her early thirties during a severe illness she experienced a series of 16 visions of our Lord. She became an anchoress, a woman dedicated to religion, living permanently alone in a cell attached to St Julian's church in Norwich; it was from this church she took the name of Julian by which we know her. For 20 years Julian mediated on her visions and recorded them in what was the first book written by a woman in English, the *Revelations of Divine Love*. This book is now recognised as one of the great classics of spiritual writing.

Readings

1 Kings 19:9-18
1 Corinthians 13:8-end
Matthew 5:13-16

Opening prayer

Lord, as we give thanks for St Julian,
we rejoice that you are our Maker, our Lover and our Keeper.
Help us to know that you abide in us and that we are in you, and that you will never let us go: we ask this in the love of Christ our Lord.

Intercessions

Loving Lord, in good and ill protect your people and keep them in your peace.
We ask your blessing upon the people of Norwich, the diocese and the bishop, for all its places of worship, especially St Julian's and St Julian's shrine.
We pray for all pilgrims and all who seek to know and love you.

We ask that we in our church and lives may be a good witness to your love.
Lord, enfolding us in love,
keep us in your peace.

Loving Lord, we give thanks for the writings of Julian and ask your blessing upon all writers.
We pray for all who seek to convey love and peace through the written word.
We ask your blessing upon all who work in conservation and the protection of species throughout our world.
We pray for areas of pollution, and the desecration of the earth, that remedies may soon be found.
Lord, enfolding us in love,
keep us in your peace.

Loving Lord, we pray for our own loved ones and friends that they may know you in their lives.
We ask your blessing upon the community in which we live.
We pray for all who teach in our schools and who influence the minds of the young.
We ask your blessing upon all who feel unloved and unwanted, and pray that we may help where we can.
Lord, enfolding us in love,
keep us in your peace.

Loving Lord, we pray for all who are tempest-tossed, all who are afflicted.
We ask your blessing upon the careworn, the weary and all who are struggling with life.
We pray for all who have fallen ill or been injured this week.
We remember (in a moment of silence) friends and loved ones who are ill.
Lord, enfolding us in love,
keep us in your peace.

Loving Lord, in this frail craft we call life, may we know you never leave us and that you will bring us to the safe haven of eternal life.

We pray for St Julian and all your saints in glory, and remember (in a moment of stillness) our loved ones departed, praying that they may enjoy the fullness of life eternal.
Merciful Father,
accept these prayers for the sake of your Son, our Saviour, Jesus Christ.
Amen.

The peace

Rest in the goodness of God,
let him reach down to the depth of your heart,
that you may abide in his peace.
The peace of the Lord be always with you.
And also with you.

Blessing

God give you grace to stand firm in the faith,
to work for his glory,
and to reveal his love:
and the blessing of God Almighty, the Father, the Son and the Holy Spirit, be upon you and remain with you always.
Amen.

19 MAY

Dunstan

Dunstan was born near Glastonbury to a noble family in 909. He received a good education, and joined the household of his uncle Athelm, Archbishop of Canterbury, and later joined the court of King Athelstan. However, in 935 he was expelled from court for studying pagan poetry and stories; he was also charged with being a magician. He was then ordained by the Bishop of Winchester and took monastic vows. He returned to Glastonbury, to live as a hermit, and practised the arts of painting, embroidery and working in metal. When Edmund became king in 939, Dunstan was recalled to court and not long after was made the Abbot of Glastonbury. He was made Bishop of Worcester in 957, then of London in 959 and finally Archbishop of Canterbury in 960. He is remembered for bringing many of the monasteries under the Benedictine Rule. He remained active as Archbishop until his death in 988.

Readings

Exodus 31:1-5
2 Corinthians 5:14-20
Matthew 18:12-24

Opening prayer

God our Creator, we give you thanks for the wisdom, talents and faithfulness of St Dunstan, for his resourcing of the monastic life and building up of the Church: may we help the Church to grow in our area by the use of our talents and our time: we ask this in the name of Christ our Lord.

Intercessions

God, giver of all good gifts, we ask your blessing upon the Church in the dioceses of Winchester, of Worcester and of Canterbury.

We ask your blessing upon all religious communities, remembering especially today the Benedictines.
We pray for all who are pastors or spiritual guides, and for those who run retreat centres.
We ask your blessing upon our church, that it may grow in faith and in number.
God of grace and goodness,
hear us and help us.

God, giver of all good gifts, we ask your blessing upon all artists, illuminators of manuscripts and workers in stained glass.
We pray for musicians, writers of music, hymn writers and all who provide us with joyous sounds.
We pray for metal workers, goldsmiths, locksmiths and jewellers, and all who beautify our world through gardening and architecture.
We remember all who strive to protect the goodness of the earth and all its creatures.
God of grace and goodness,
hear us and help us.

God, giver of all good gifts, we ask your blessing upon all who strive to build up and make our community beautiful and welcoming.
We pray for all who look after parks and public places and care for their safety.
We remember the work of the local police, medical staff and social workers.
We pray for our homes and our loved ones, that we may use the talents you have given to us.
God of grace and goodness,
hear us and help us.

God, giver of all good gifts, we pray for all whose sight is impaired and for those who suffer from blindness.
We ask your blessing upon the work of opticians and eye surgeons, remembering the work of the Royal National Institute of Blind People, and Sightsavers.
We pray for all who have lost vision of the goodness of God and the beauty of his creation.

We pray for all who are ill or in need of help (in a moment of silence we pray for any known to us).
God of grace and goodness,
hear us and help us.

God, giver of all good gifts, we give thanks for the life and witness of St Dunstan and his working for your glory.
We pray for those who have died recently . . . and (in a moment of stillness) we pray for our loved ones departed.
Merciful Father,
accept these prayers for the sake of your Son, our Saviour, Jesus Christ. Amen.

The peace

Let us make every effort to maintain the unity of the Spirit in the bond of peace.
The peace of the Lord be always with you.
And also with you.

Blessing

The joy of God the Creator,
the love of Christ the Saviour,
the power of the Holy Spirit be upon you:
and the blessing of God Almighty, the Father, the Son and the Holy Spirit, be upon you and remain with you always.
Amen.

20 MAY

Alcuin

Alcuin was born in York, about 735, of an ancient Northumbrian family. Entering the cathedral school as a child, he finally became the Master of the school. In 781 he went to Aachen as Master of the Palace School and adviser on religion and education to the court of Charlemagne: it was here he set up an important library at the palace. Although he was not a monk and only a deacon, he was made Abbot of Tours in 796. In a letter about the sack of Holy Island in 793, he describes Lindisfarne as the 'holiest place in Britain'. He also exhorts the survivors, 'Let us love what is eternal, and not what is perishable. Let us esteem true riches, not fleeting ones, eternal not transitory ones.'

Readings

Isaiah 61:10–62. 5
Colossians 3:12-16
John 4:19-24

Opening prayer

Lord of light, as we give thanks for St Alcuin, we ask that your eternal light may shine in our lives and disperse all darkness and coldness, that we may serve you with all our heart and mind and strength: we ask this in love of him who is the Light of the World, Jesus Christ our Lord.

Intercessions

Eternal Goodness, as we give thanks for St Alcuin, we pray for York Minster, the Minster School, and the Archbishop of York.
We ask your blessing upon the Church and people of Tours and of Aachen.

We pray for those who provide us with new prayers, prayer books and liturgies.
We give thanks for those who have taught us to pray and ask that we remain faithful to their teaching.
Eternal Love,
hear us and help us.

Eternal Goodness, we give you thanks for all writers, poets, printers and publishers, for all who provide us with reading material.
We ask your blessing upon the media and all who work in publishing and the provision of daily news.
We pray for those who have learning difficulties, that they may be helped as much as possible.
We give thanks for dedicated teachers and for all who help in the process of our learning.
Eternal Love,
hear us and help us.

Eternal Goodness, we remember before you homes where there are tensions and difficulties.
We pray for families where relationships are suffering from a breakdown in love or communication.
We remember all homeless people, and those separated from loved ones.
We give thanks for our own homes and loved ones and ask your blessing of peace upon us.
Eternal Love,
hear us and help us.

Eternal Goodness, we pray for all who walk in darkness.
We ask your blessing upon the depressed and the despairing, that they may come to your light and know your love.
We pray for homes where there is illness and for the ability of the family to cope.
We pray for friends and loved ones who are ill (and in a time of stillness, remember them by name).
Eternal Love,
hear us and help us.

Eternal Goodness, we give thanks that in your love, life is eternal.
We rejoice in the fellowship of St Alcuin and all your saints in glory.
We remember our loved ones and friends departed (and in silence name them before you).
Merciful Father,
accept these prayers for the sake of your Son, our Saviour, Jesus Christ.
Amen.

The peace

The eternal light shine in the darkness of our lives,
the eternal goodness delver us from evil,
and guide our feet into the way of peace.
The peace of the Lord be always with you.
And also with you.

Blessing

The grace and goodness of God
deliver you from all evil;
the power of God be your strength:
and the blessing of God Almighty, the Father, the Son and the Holy Spirit, be upon you and remain with you always.
Amen.

24 MAY

John and Charles Wesley

The brothers John and Charles Wesley were sons of an Anglican priest and brought up at Epworth Rectory. John, who was ordained as a priest, went through a conversion experience in 1738: he described it as feeling his heart 'strangely warmed'. After this, often accompanied by his brother Charles, he became an itinerant preacher travelling around the country. He built up worship groups which were to become the seeds of the Methodist Church. Though the brothers remained within the Anglican Church all their lives, the Methodist Church spread worldwide after their death. Charles left a wonderful legacy of thousands of hymns, many of which enrich the Church to this day.

Readings

Isaiah 6:1-8
Ephesians 5:5-12
John 21:20-25

Opening prayer

God of grace, we thank you for the music, mission and ministry of John and Charles Wesley and that their hearts were warmed by an awareness of you and your love. We pray that our hearts also may be warmed and our lives filled with love for you and your world: we ask this in the name of Christ our Lord.

Intercessions

Love Divine, we give you thanks for the love that made John and Charles Wesley seek to reach out in mission in word and music.
Lord, kindle in us the fire of your love and send us out to proclaim your presence.
We pray for all church musicians, hymn writers, preachers, and teachers of the faith.

We ask your blessing upon the Methodist Church and its share in worldwide ministry.
Eternal Love,
hear us, and have mercy upon us.

Love Divine, we pray that we may all find our true purpose and serve you with joy.
We pray for all who are unemployed and whose talents are frustrated.
We ask your blessing upon all who have been made to feel useless.
We pray for refugees, displaced persons and all who live in shanty towns or on the streets.
Eternal Love,
hear us, and have mercy upon us.

Love Divine, help us to help each other, to give a hand and to be aware of each other's needs.
May we be aware of the needs within the communities to which we belong, and help where we can.
We ask your blessing upon all home visitors and carers.
We pray for our own homes, loved ones and our neighbours.
Eternal Love,
hear us, and have mercy upon us.

Love Divine, we ask your blessing upon all who suffer from dementia or Alzheimer's disease and for those caring for them.
We pray for all those who can no longer cope on their own, and those who feel they are a burden to others.
We ask your blessing upon the hospice movement and all who care for the terminally ill.
We pray for friends and loved ones who are suffering in any way, for their wellbeing and peace. (In a moment of silence, let us name them before God.)
Eternal Love,
hear us, and have mercy upon us.

Love Divine, we give thanks for all those lives in whom your love has burned brightly, remembering today John and Charles Wesley.

We pray for our loved ones departed, that they may find rest in you and eternal life in your presence.
Merciful Father,
accept these prayers for the sake of your Son, our Saviour, Jesus Christ.
Amen.

The peace

Live in the peace of Christ,
in joy reveal his presence.
Let the peace of Christ fill your hearts and minds.
The peace of the Lord be always with you.
And also with you.

Blessing

God give you a warm heart to love him,
a tender heart towards all his creation,
and a faithful heart to abide in him:
and the blessing of God Almighty, the Father, the Son and the Holy Spirit, be upon you and remain with you always.
Amen.

25 MAY

Bede

Bede was born on lands owned by the monks of St Peter's Wearmouth c.672–3. When he was seven, he was entrusted into the care of Abbot Benedict of St Peter's for his education. He spent the rest of his life in this community. He later moved, with Coelfrith his tutor and now his abbot, to St Paul's Jarrow, a new foundation and consecrated by Archbishop Theodore. When he was 19, Bede was made a deacon, and a priest at the age of 30. The twin foundations were rich in art, music and manuscripts brought back by Abbot Benedict from his pilgrimages to Rome. Bede had a great interest in the world; he described how the earth was a globe and had five zones, two cold, two temperate and one hot. He taught himself to measure the latitudes of the world. He also showed how the rise and fall of the river Tyne with the tides were caused by the phases of the moon. He hardly ever left the monastery. He went to Lindisfarne once when he was writing *The Life of St Cuthbert*, and once to York to visit a former pupil who was now the Bishop of York. He wrote commentaries on and translated the Scriptures. But he is best remembered for his *Ecclesiastical History of the English People*. He died in 735, after just finishing dictating the translation of St John's Gospel to a scribe.

Readings

Ecclesiasticus 39:1-10
1 Corinthians 1:18-25
John 21:20-25

Opening prayer

Lord God, we give you thanks for the life as monk and writings of the Venerable Bede, especially for his account of the Church in this land from its beginnings and up to his life-time. May we learn from our past and respect the rich heritage which can teach us much: we ask this in the name of Christ our Lord.

Intercessions

Lord of light, we give you thanks for calling Bede to be a faithful scribe and a recorder of the history of the English Church and people.
We ask your blessing upon the churches of St Peter's Wearmouth, St Paul's Jarrow and the Cathedral Church of Durham.
We pray for all religious communities and places of retreat, remembering especially . . .
We pray that the church to which we belong will be a witness to your love by its prayer and its outreach.
Compassionate God,
hear us and help us.

Lord of light, we remember all who live in the darkness of fear or the threat of violence.
We pray for war-torn areas and for all who have lost loved ones or their homes.
We ask your blessing upon all children who have been separated from their parents and for the work of Save the Children.
We pray for our land, for Elizabeth our Queen and for our government.
Compassionate God,
hear us and help us.

Lord of light, we give thanks for all who have revealed your love to us.
We ask your blessing upon our homes, our friends and the communities to which we belong.
We pray for all places of education and for all who help to guide and teach our children.
We pray for people who are new to our area and are seeking friendship and guidance.
Compassionate God,
hear us and help us.

Lord of light, we ask your blessing upon all whose lives are darkened by chronic illness or failing abilities.
We pray for those who suffer from unemployment, poverty or hunger.
We remember friends and loved ones who are ill (and in the silence name them before you).

We ask your blessing upon all who work in hospitals and assist in healing.
Compassionate God,
hear us and help us.

Lord of light, we give you thanks for the inspiration of Bede and pray that he may rejoice with your saints in glory.
We remember all who have died this week and pray for . . .
and (in a moment of stillness) ask that our loved ones departed may enjoy the fullness of life in your kingdom.
Merciful Father,
accept these prayers for the sake of your Son, our Saviour, Jesus Christ.
Amen.

The peace

The Good Shepherd in love seeks those who are near and those who are far off to enfold them in his power and his peace.
The peace of the Lord be always with you.
And also with you.

Blessing

The mighty God, who is able to keep you in life eternal, is with you.
The Christ, who upholds all who walk in darkness, is with you.
The Holy Spirit, who renews and refreshes you, is with you:
and the blessing of God Almighty, the Father, the Son and the Holy Spirit, be upon you and remain with you always.
Amen.

26 MAY

Augustine of Canterbury

Augustine was born in Italy. He became a monk and then the Prior of St Andrew's Monastery in Rome. In 596 he was chosen by Pope Gregory to head a mission, with a group of monks, to England. While on the way in Gaul he would have turned back, but for the encouragement of Pope Gregory. They landed at Ebbsfleet in Kent in 597 and were cautiously received by King Ethelbert, who gave them a house in Canterbury and allowed them to preach. By 601 Ethelbert and many of his people had been baptised, and more clergy were sent from Rome. Augustine returned to Gaul to be consecrated as bishop. Augustine built the first cathedral in Canterbury and consolidated his mission around this area. He founded the monastery of St Peter and St Paul, later to be called St Augustine's, just outside the city walls; he also founded a school and scriptorium. He created another see at Rochester and later another based in London. As the first Archbishop of Canterbury, he died about the year 604.

Readings

Ezekiel 3:16-21
1 Thessalonians 2:2b-8
Matthew 13:31-33

Opening prayer

Lord God, we rejoice that you called St Augustine to preach and teach the people of this land the way to the life which is eternal. May we who share in the fruits of his labour work for a respect for the earth, a restoring faith and a deep love for you our Creator: we ask this in the love of Christ our Lord.

Intercessions

God our Creator, we pray for all who proclaim your presence within and love for creation.
We ask your blessing upon the dioceses of Rochester and London, and the archdiocese of Canterbury, and pray for all who live within that area.
We pray for all who go out in mission, for evangelists, preachers and teachers, and that they may encourage us to love and care for all of creation.
We pray for scientists and ecologists who seek to show that this world is full of the mystery of your presence.
Lord of all creation,
hear us and renew us.

God our Creator, we ask your blessing upon all leaders of people and those who influence the minds of others.
We pray for the leaders of industry and the great multi-nationals, that they may work with integrity and sensitivity towards all of your creation.
Grant that we may show the same sensitivity and compassion for the earth and its creatures.
We pray for lives that have been ruined through the greed and hard-heartedness of others.
Lord of all creation,
hear us and renew us.

God our Creator, we pray for areas where family life is being eroded and communities destroyed.
We remember areas where people are struggling to survive and are in great need.
We pray for all who work with loving care and compassion for others.
We give thanks for our homes and loved ones and ask your blessing upon them.
Lord of all creation,
hear us and renew us.

God our Creator, we pray for areas of the world where there is serious pollution or where people do not have fresh water.
We remember the many people who are without medical services or proper medicines.

We give thanks for the hospitals and medical services of our land and ask your blessing upon them.
We pray for all who are troubled or ill (and in a moment of silence we bring before you those whom we know).
Lord of all creation,
hear us and renew us.

God our Creator, we rejoice in the fellowship of St Augustine and all your saints who have responded to your call of love.
We ask your blessing upon our loved ones departed from us (and in the stillness name them before you), praying that we may share with them in your eternal kingdom.
Merciful Father,
accept these prayers for the sake of your Son, our Saviour, Jesus Christ. Amen.

The peace

Make every effort to maintain the unity of the Spirit, in the bond of peace.
The peace of the Lord be always with you.
And also with you.

Blessing

The Lord warm your heart with the fire of his love,
lighten your path with the light of his presence,
enfold you in his peace:
and the blessing of God Almighty, the Father, the Son and the Holy Spirit, be upon you and remain with you always.
Amen.

30 MAY

Josephine Butler

Josephine Butler (née Grey) was born in Northumberland in 1828. She married an Anglican priest in 1852. Throughout her life she was a devout Christian and a woman of prayer. Her spirituality was much influenced by the teachings of St Catherine of Siena, whose biography she wrote. She was appalled by the treatment of prostitutes, many of whom had been forced by poverty to take up that way of life. She set up a House of Rest and an Industrial Home for women she had rescued from prostitution. From 1869 she worked and spoke out not only at home but in Europe against the way these women were treated. Finally, in 1883 her work led to the repealing of the Contagious Diseases Act, which had stigmatised women in the way they were treated

Readings

Isaiah 58:6-11
1 John 3:18-23
Matthew 9:10-13

Opening prayer

Loving Father, we thank you for the life and work of Josephine Butler in her concern for those in need of help. As we remember her work to fight against injustice and the abuse of oppressed women, help us to stand for freedom and justice at all times and to reveal your love, our Maker and Redeemer, for all of your creation: we ask this in the name of Christ our Lord.

Intercessions

Lord of life and love, we give thanks for the life and work of Josephine Butler, for her bravery and her love.
We pray for all who risk their lives to gain freedom and fullness of life for others.

We ask your blessing upon those who seek to live the gospel and serve Christ in the poor and rejected.
We pray for those who are rejected themselves because of the work they do among outcasts and oppressed people.
Compassionate God,
hear our prayer.

Lord of life and love, we pray for oppressed peoples throughout the world, and all who are denied freedom because of their gender or colour.
We ask your blessing upon all who work in government and in the emergency services to relieve poverty and suffering.
We pray for places of sanctuary and safe houses, where people can escape from abuse or violence, and can find compassion and rest.
We pray for all who are forced to live on the streets due to poverty or homelessness.
Compassionate God,
hear our prayer.

Lord of life and love, we give thanks for our loved ones who have enriched our lives by their love and care.
We ask your blessing upon our families, friends and the communities to which we belong.
We pray for all who enrich our lives through art, music, and writing; and pray for all who work in broadcasting.
We pray for all young people leaving home and especially those whose lives may be endangered.
Compassionate God,
hear our prayer.

We pray for all who feel lost or unable to cope with life and for those who care for them.
We remember all who live in depressed areas, poverty or squalid surroundings.
We pray for all who are working to improve the situation of refugees.
We pray for all who are ill (and in a time of quiet remember friends, neighbours and loved ones in their troubles).
Lord of life and love, we remember all who have given their lives in the service of others.

We pray for those who have recently died and those who are bereaved.
We remember our own friends and loved ones departed from us . . .
Merciful Father,
accept these prayers for the sake of your Son, our Saviour, Jesus Christ.
Amen.

The peace

Know that in the compassion of God there is forgiveness, healing, strength and peace.
The peace of the Lord be always with you.
And also with you.

Blessing

God give you a warm heart to love him,
a kind heart to reveal him,
a compassionate heart to serve him,
a faithful heart to abide in him:
and the blessing of God Almighty, the Father, the Son and the Holy Spirit, be upon you and remain with you always.
Amen.

JUNE

1 JUNE

Justin Martyr

Justin was born in Palestine of a pagan family at the beginning of the second century. As a young man, he studied various beliefs and philosophies before becoming a Christian at the age of 30. He taught Christianity as a philosophy at Ephesus and later at Rome. He became an outstanding defender of the Christian faith and is remembered as one of the first thinkers to enter into a serious dialogue with other intellectual disciplines, including Judaism. He constantly sought to reconcile the claims of faith and reason. About the year 165 he and some of his followers were denounced as Christians and beheaded. The record of their martyrdom is in an official court report which has survived. It is by tradition that he is given the title Martyr.

Readings

1 Maccabees 2:15-22
1 Corinthians 1:18-25
John 15:18-21

Opening prayer

God, giver of life and life eternal, we give you thanks for all who have been faithful witnesses to you in word and deed, and remember especially today Justin Martyr. May we stand firm in our faith and witness in our lives to your saving love: we ask this in the name of Christ our Lord.

Intercessions

Lord of life eternal, we give thanks for Justin and all your faithful people.
We ask your blessing upon all who remain faithful to you in difficult and dangerous places.

We remember all who are being persecuted for their faith, and those struggling with doubt and despair.
We pray for all seeking to strengthen their faith and to love you more.
Lord, our hope and joy,
hear us and help us.

Lord of life eternal, we pray for all who are in places of power: rulers, governments, multi-international firms, and large industries.
We remember all who have spoken out against malpractice and have suffered for it.
We pray for a sensitivity towards our planet in our use of resources and in our farming methods.
We ask your blessing upon all who speak out for the poor and the oppressed of our world.
Lord, our hope and joy,
hear us and help us.

Lord of life eternal, we remember all who have shared their faith with us and helped us to know and love you.
We ask your blessing upon all who are teachers and preachers.
We pray for our families and friends, for their safety and their peace.
In all our relationships may we reveal your compassion and care.
Lord, our hope and joy,
hear us and help us.

Lord of life eternal, we remember all who are being persecuted or marginalised throughout the world.
We remember all who feel betrayed or let down by the society they live in.
We pray for all who are denied justice or freedom of speech.
We ask your blessing upon all who are ill (and in a moment of stillness we bring before God those known to us).
Lord, our hope and joy,
hear us and help us.

Lord of life eternal, in you alone is our hope and peace.
We give you thanks for all your saints and holy martyrs, remembering especially Justin.

We pray for our loved ones departed, that they may rejoice with your saints in glory.
Merciful Father,
accept these prayers for the sake of your Son, our Saviour, Jesus Christ.
Amen.

The peace

Do not be afraid, rest in God who is eternal
and abide in his love and peace.
The peace of the Lord be always with you.
And also with you.

Blessing

God's presence surround you,
God's power protect you,
God's peace dwell within you:
and the blessing of God Almighty, the Father, the Son and the Holy Spirit, be upon you and remain with you always.
Amen.

5 JUNE

Boniface

Boniface was born Winfrith, at Crediton in Devon about the year 675. He took the name Boniface when he entered the monastery in Exeter as a young man. He became a Latin scholar, a schoolmaster and poet. When he was 30 he was ordained priest. In 716 he went as a missionary to Frisia. He was consecrated bishop by the Pope to work in Hesse and Bavaria in 722. At Geismar he felled the sacred oak and challenged the pagan gods to defend it. As they did not and no ill befell him, many conversions followed. He founded a group of monasteries across southern Germany. He made sure they were places of education and evangelism. In 732 he became the Archbishop of Mainz and from there consecrated many other missionary bishops, also helping to reform the Church in France. When almost 80, he returned to Frisia and was martyred by some pagans in 754.

Readings

Jonah 3:1-5
Acts 20:24-28
Luke 10:1-9

Opening prayer

Gracious God, as we give thanks for Boniface and his proclaiming of the gospel to the German peoples, teach us to give ourselves in your service and to draw others to be aware of your steadfast love and saving power: we ask this in the name of our Saviour, Jesus Christ.

Intercessions

Lord of love, we give you thanks and praise for the life and witness of Boniface.
We pray for the Church in Germany and the Archbishop of Mainz: in this land we pray for the diocese of Exeter, its bishop and the people of Devon.

We ask your blessing upon all who serve you in religious orders and in missionary societies.
We pray for all who are new to the faith, that they may be encouraged and strengthened.
Lord of light,
hear us and guide us.

Lord of love, we ask your blessing upon all places of learning remembering especially . . .
We pray for students and teachers, as minds are influenced and patterns formed.
We ask your blessing and guidance upon the media, as it can affect us all.
We pray that all who are in power may use their talents with care and respect for the earth and its people.
Lord of light,
hear us and guide us.

Lord of love, we give thanks for our homes and loved ones and ask your blessing upon them.
We ask your blessing upon all who provide for the needs of our area and all who work within the community.
We pray for those who provide relaxation, refreshment and entertainment.
Lord, may we be useful and productive members of our homes and our communities.
Lord of light,
hear us and guide us.

Lord of love, we pray for all who are fearful and anxious about life.
We remember those awaiting a doctor's diagnosis or who are waiting to go into hospital.
We ask your blessing upon the hospice movement and those who are terminally ill.
We pray for friends, neighbours and loved ones who are ill at this time . . .
Lord of light,
hear us and guide us.

Lord of love, we rejoice that, in you, death is not the end but the gateway to life eternal.
We give thanks for Boniface and all your saints in glory.
(In a time of stillness) we pray for our loved ones departed . . .
Merciful Father,
accept these prayers for the sake of your Son, our Saviour, Jesus Christ.
Amen.

The peace

Christ the Good Shepherd, in love, seeks those who are near and those who are far off to enfold in his grace and peace.
The peace of the Lord be always with you.
And also with you.

Blessing

The joy of God the Creator,
the love of Christ the Saviour,
the power of the Holy Spirit
go with you, strengthen and guide you:
and the blessing of God Almighty, the Father, the Son and the Holy Spirit, be upon you and remain with you always.
Amen.

8 JUNE

Thomas Ken

Thomas Ken was born in 1637 at Little Berkhampstead, Hertfordshire. He was educated at New College, Oxford, and was priested in 1662. His ministry was in the Winchester diocese until he became chaplain to King Charles II. Later he became the Bishop of Bath and Wells. He wrote many hymns, including the morning hymn 'Awake my soul' and the evening hymn 'Glory to Thee, my God, this night'. He was not happy with the reforms of James II, but when William and Mary succeeded James II he felt unable to take the oath against the king he saw as his anointed monarch, so was counted among the non-jurors. He died in 1711.

Readings

Malachi 2:5-7
2 Corinthians 4:1-10
Matthew 24:42-46

Opening prayer

God, from whom all blessings flow, we give you thanks and praise for the ministry and hymn writing of Thomas Ken. As with him, may we awake to your presence each day and give you glory each night: we ask this in the love of Christ our Lord.

Intercessions

God, giver of all good gifts, we give thanks for all who have provided us with hymns and music.
We ask your blessing upon all hymn writers, poets and musicians.
We pray for all pastors and shepherds of your people, and remember those who have stood firm in their faith against all opposition and persecution.

As we give thanks for Thomas Ken, we pray for the diocese of Bath and Wells and all who live in its area.
Keep us, O King of kings,
beneath the shadow of your wings.

God, giver of all good gifts, we ask your blessing upon this land, upon Elizabeth our Queen and our government.
We pray for all leaders of people and for all who are in positions of great power, that they may have sensitivity towards and care for those in their charge.
We pray for all areas of unrest, war, flood or famine, and for all who have had to leave their homes and possessions.
We remember small communities of indigenous peoples who are endangered by large corporations in pursuit of resources.
Keep us, O King of kings,
beneath the shadow of your wings.

God, giver of all good gifts, we give thanks for all who help our young people to develop their talents and abilities.
We pray for any who feel frustrated through lack of opportunity to work or through disability.
We pray for the communities to which we belong, that they may be caring for and encouraging people in their lives.
We ask your blessing upon our homes and our loved ones.
Keep us, O King of kings,
beneath the shadow of your wings.

God, giver of all good gifts, we give thanks for all healers and bringers of peace.
We pray for the peace-keeping forces of our world and for all relief agencies.
We ask your blessing upon all who have been marginalised and ignored by the society in which they live, especially those who are now despairing of life.
We remember all who are ill (and in a moment of stillness bring before God those dear to us).
Keep us, O King of kings,
beneath the shadow of your wings.

God, giver of all good gifts, we give thanks for all your blessings in our lives and pray that, when we from death shall wake, we may of endless life partake.
We pray for all our loved ones departed (remembering those dear to us).
Merciful Father,
accept these prayers for the sake of your Son, our Saviour, Jesus Christ.
Amen.

The peace

The light of the Lord shine upon you and guide you,
that you may walk in the way of life and of peace.
The peace of the Lord be always with you.
And also with you.

Blessing

Know that the Lord is your stronghold and deliverer,
he is your strength and shield;
put your trust in him always:
and the blessing of God Almighty, the Father, the Son and the Holy Spirit, be upon you and remain with you always.
Amen.

9 JUNE

Columba

Columba was born at Garten of the royal Ui Neill clan in 521. He trained as a monk under Finnian of Moville and then under Finnian of Clonard. Later he founded the monasteries of Derry (546), Durrow (c.556) and possibly Kells. In 565 he left Ireland with 12 companions for Iona, where he founded the monastery and was its first Abbot. From there the monks went out in mission. Columba converted Brude the king of the Picts, founding two churches in Inverness. In 574 Aidan, the Irish king of Dalriada, was consecrated by him. He was said to be a striking figure but also quite austere at times. Most of his influence in his life-time was in the Western Isles. He died in 597.

Readings

Isaiah 61:1-3
Titus 2:11-end
Luke 12:32-37

Opening prayer

Dear Lord, we give you praise for the life of Columba, and pray that you will go before us to guide us, be a kindly shepherd behind us, be beneath us to uphold us, and above us to raise us up: we ask this in the name of Christ our Lord.

Intercessions

Lord of life, as Columba in joy showed a compassion and care for those around him, grant that our lives may show the joy of knowing you, and show our care for all.
As Columba founded the monasteries of Derry, Durrow and Kells, we pray for the Church in Ireland and for all who are called to the religious life.

As Columba founded the community on Iona, we pray for the island and its people, for the work of the Iona Community and for Bishop's House.
We ask your blessing upon all places of pilgrimage and all pilgrim people.
God, holy and strong One,
we put our trust in you.

Lord of life, we ask your blessing upon all artists, musicians and crafts people.
We pray for those who use their talents for the benefit of all creation.
We remember research scientists and those who work in conservation.
We pray for the Scottish parliament and the people of Scotland.
We remember all who live in small and scattered communities and are finding it hard to make a living.
God, holy and strong One,
we put our trust in you.

Lord of life, we give thanks for the heritage of our country, and for all who have built it up.
We pray for all who care for the soil and who produce food for us to eat.
We ask your blessing upon all who labour that we may be provided for, and we remember any who do not get a fair deal.
We pray for our loved ones and friends, that we may all live in joy and peace.
God, holy and strong One,
we put our trust in you.

Lord of life, we remember all whose lives are restricted through poverty or prejudice.
We pray for all who suffer from a disability and are restricted in what they can do.
We pray that we may all help each other in times of need.
We ask your blessing upon all who are ill or struggling with life (and in a moment of silence we name those known to us before God).
God, holy and strong One,
we put our trust in you.

Lord of life, we rejoice in the fellowship of Columba and all your saints. We pray that our loved ones departed may rejoice in the communion of saints in your eternal kingdom (and in the silence we remember them by name).
Merciful Father,
accept these prayers for the sake of your Son, our Saviour, Jesus Christ.
Amen.

The peace

The Lord holds us fast in love,
enfolds us in his protection,
and surrounds us with his peace.
The peace of the Lord be always with you.
And also with you.

Blessing

The Lord be a bright light before you,
a sure path beneath you,
a kindly shepherd behind you,
and a strong hand above you to raise you up:
and the blessing of God Almighty, the Father, the Son and the Holy Spirit, be upon you and remain with you always.
Amen.

16 JUNE

Richard of Chichester

Richard was born at a Droitwich in 1197, the son of a yeoman farmer. He worked hard on the farm for a few years as a young man. He was then able to study at Oxford, Paris and Bologna. He returned to Oxford as its chancellor, and then became the chancellor to the Archbishop of Canterbury. He went to France in exile with his Archbishop and there studied with the Dominicans and was ordained priest in 1242. In 1244 he was elected as Bishop of Chichester. Richard returned to his bishop's properties in Chichester but they were very dilapidated as they had been confiscated by Henry III. Richard lived at Tarring in the parish priest's house and visited his diocese on foot. Contemporaries hailed him as a model bishop who was accessible. Near the end of his life he was prominent in preaching the Crusade. He fell ill while at Dover recruiting for the Crusades and died there in 1253. He is the author of the well-loved prayer: 'Thanks be to Thee, Lord Jesus Christ, for all the benefits Thou hast given me, for all the pains and insults Thou hast born for me. O most merciful redeemer, friend and brother, may I know Thee more clearly, love Thee more dearly and follow Thee more nearly, day by day.'

Readings

Jeremiah 1:4-10
1 Peter 5:1-4
John 21:15-19

Opening prayer

Dear Lord, we give you thanks and praise for Richard of Chichester, remembering his love for the poor and his life of prayer. With him we pray that we may know you more clearly, love you more dearly, and follow you more nearly, day by day: we ask this in the name of Christ our Saviour.

Intercessions

Dear Lord, we give thanks for Richard of Chichester and ask your blessing upon the people and diocese of Chichester.
We pray for all pastoral visitors and for those who take the sacraments to the infirm and the ill.
We remember the work of hospital chaplains.
We pray that we may be good stewards of all that you have given to us.
In your love and mercy,
hear us and help us.

Dear Lord, we pray that we may live simply that others may simply live.
We ask that we may all learn a more caring and respectful approach to the earth and its resources.
We remember all who do not receive a fair wage and those who are used as cheap labour.
We pray for indigenous peoples whose way of life and traditions are under threat.
In your love and mercy,
hear us and help us.

Dear Lord, we give thanks for all the blessings you have given to us, our homes and our loved ones: may we appreciate what we have.
We pray for all who maintain and care for the upkeep of the communities to which we belong.
We ask your blessing upon the local council and pray for all who work within government.
We pray that our communities may work together in harmony and peace.
In your love and mercy,
hear us and help us.

Dear Lord, we remember all who are struggling in life or in their care of a loved one or neighbour.
We ask your blessing upon social and relief workers and upon those in their care.
We pray for all who act as friendly neighbours towards each other in times of need.

We pray for all who are ill or distressed at this time (and in a moment of silence, we bring to God those whom we know).
In your love and mercy,
hear us and help us.

Dear Lord, we give thanks for all that Jesus has done for us, for all that he has borne for us, and pray that we may love him more dearly.
We pray for Richard of Chichester, that he may rejoice in glory.
We pray for friends and loved ones departed (and name them before God).
Merciful Father,
accept these prayers for the sake of your Son, our Saviour, Jesus Christ. Amen.

The peace

The Lord of life give you peace,
in your hearts,
in your minds,
and in all your lives.
The peace of the Lord be always with you.
And also with you.

Blessing

The God of grace and goodness, who is ever present,
guide you,
support you,
and keep you in his love:
and the blessing of God Almighty, the Father, the Son and the Holy Spirit, be upon you and remain with you always.
Amen.

22 JUNE

Alban

Alban lived in the third century at Verulamium, which was later to be name St Albans. He is the first martyr we know of in what was to become England. Few details are known about him. It is believed that Alban was a Roman soldier who sheltered a Christian priest during one of the persecutions and was converted by him. Those in search of the priest were sent to Alban's house. Alban dressed in the priest's cloak to enable the priest to escape. He was arrested and, after refusing to offer sacrifice to the Roman gods, was sentenced to death. It is said one executioner was converted, and it took another to put him to death. He is a reminder of the bravery and witness of the early Christians in this land.

Readings

Wisdom 4:10-15
2 Timothy 2:3-7
John 12:24-26

Opening prayer

Father, we give you thanks for Alban, who gave his life to save another, and in so doing became the first martyr we know of in this land: may we follow his example of love for others in the way we live our lives and witness to the love of Christ our Saviour: we ask this in the love of him who died for us, Jesus Christ our Lord.

Intercessions

Lord of love, we give thanks for the life and sacrifice of Alban.
We pray for the diocese and the people of St Albans and their witness to Christ our Saviour.

May the whole Church be generous in its giving of itself and in its care of all in need of shelter.
We remember areas of the world where people are still being persecuted for their faith: and pray today especially for . . .
Lord, in your loving kindness,
hear us and help us.

Lord of love, we pray for all who risk their lives in the care and service of others.
We ask your blessing upon those who care for and protect minorities and people in danger of oppression.
We pray for the peacemakers and peace-keeping forces throughout the world.
We remember all whose lives are endangered because they are defending and protecting others.
Lord, in your loving kindness,
hear us and help us.

Lord of love, we give you thanks for our loved ones who quietly sacrifice for us, and pray that we may give ourselves for them.
Lord, as we have received, make us generous in our giving.
We pray for all who sustain our society by the giving of their time and talents.
We remember before you any who are in need of care and attention in our community.
Lord, in your loving kindness,
hear us and help us.

Lord of love, we pray for all who are suffering, due to their caring for or protection of others.
We pray for those who seek to protect endangered species and the rain forests.
May we learn to walk gently on the earth and not waste resources, or neglect the needy.
We ask your blessing upon all who are ill or suffering in any way (we remember those known to us, in a time of quiet).
Lord, in your loving kindness,
hear us and help us.

Lord of love, we give thanks for the gift of eternal life and the power of the resurrection.
We give thanks for St Alban and pray for all who have died in the service of their country and their God.
As we remember all the faithful departed, we pray for those who are dear to us and are in God's keeping.
Merciful Father,
accept these prayers for the sake of your Son, our Saviour, Jesus Christ.
Amen.

The peace

Know that the Lord is your strength and salvation,
in him is your peace.
The peace of the Lord be always with you.
And also with you.

Blessing

God give you the light of his presence to guide you,
his strength to support you,
his love to lead you:
and the blessing of God Almighty, the Father, the Son and the Holy Spirit, be upon you and remain with you always.
Amen.

23 JUNE

Etheldreda

Etheldreda was the daughter of Anna, the king of East Anglia. At an early age she married c.652 but remained a virgin. Her husband died three years later. She then retired to the Isle of Ely. In 660, for political reasons, she was again married, this time to Egfrith, King of Northumbria, who was only 15. At her wish she remained a virgin. But 12 years later, the king realised he needed to have a son to follow him. Etheldreda refused and, with the help of Bishop Wilfrid, became a nun at Coldingham, where her aunt Ebba was the abbess. In 673 she left there to found a double monastery on her lands in Ely. There she spent seven years living an austere life, eating only one meal a day, often keeping early morning vigils and spending time in prayer. She died in 679. A fair was held at Ely annually in her memory. She was often known as Audrey and the cheap things of the fair were known as 'tawdries'.

Readings

Song of Solomon 8:6, 7
Acts 4:32-35
Matthew 25:1-13

Opening prayer

Almighty Father, we give you thanks and praise for the life and example of Etheldreda, who turned her back on riches to devote her life more fully to you and to care for those in need. Grant that we may also seek you, where true riches are to be found and in whom is peace and life eternal: we ask this in the love of Christ our Lord.

Intercessions

Compassionate God, as we praise you for Etheldreda, we ask your blessing upon the people and the diocese of Ely.
We pray for all who have joined religious communities, and for those who have dedicated their lives to the care of the poor and the needy.
We ask your blessing upon all who teach us to pray, through example, word or teaching.
We pray for our own lives of prayer and service to others: that our church may grow in faith and in number.
Giver of all good gifts,
hear our prayers.

Compassionate God, we ask your blessing upon all who help people to improve their lives.
We pray for teachers and tutors, for musicians and artists, for craftspeople and gardeners.
We pray for all town and city planners, that they may respect the land and deal carefully with the environment.
We give thanks for all who have inspired us, and pray we may inspire others.
Giver of all good gifts,
hear our prayers.

Compassionate God, we pray that our homes may be homes of peace and love.
May we know that the true riches are the people around us, and live together in joy.
We pray for those obsessed by riches, and remember also those who do not have enough to survive healthily.
We ask your blessing upon the community to which we belong and pray that it may have a clear vision of its priorities.
Giver of all good gifts,
hear our prayers.

Compassionate God, we pray for all who are in relationships that are not good for their wellbeing.
We pray for those who are caught up in addictions or vice, and those who feel they have become captives to a lower way of life.

We pray for our local homes, hospitals and hospices in their care and compassion for others.
We pray for all who are ill or suffering in any way (and in a time of silence we bring before God those we know).
Giver of all good gifts,
hear our prayers.

Compassionate God,
we give thanks for Etheldreda and all your saints in glory.
We remember those who have died this week, especially . . .
(and in a moment of stillness, pray for our loved ones departed).
Merciful Father,
accept these prayers for the sake of your Son, our Saviour, Jesus Christ.
Amen.

The peace

Walk gently upon the earth,
treat all beings with respect,
seek to live in peace with all.
The peace of the Lord be always with you.
And also with you.

Blessing

God give you grace to follow the example of his saints,
to be compassionate,
to show forgiveness and mercy,
to live in love and peace:
and the blessing of God Almighty, the Father, the Son and the Holy Spirit, be upon you and remain with you always.
Amen.

28 JUNE

Irenaeus

Irenaeus was born about the year 130, probably at Smyrna where he heard Polycarp the Bishop preach when he was a boy. As Polycarp had been a disciple of the Apostle John, it was a link to the early apostolic Church. Irenaeus studied at Rome, and later became a priest at Lyons in Gaul. When the Bishop of Lyons was martyred in 177, Irenaeus was consecrated as the new bishop. He took a firm stand against the Gnostics, and emphasised the full humanity of Jesus Christ. He saw part of the work of a bishop was to stand firm against heresies and false doctrine. He drew upon the traditions of both East and West. He is honoured as the first great Catholic theologian. He died about the year 200.

Readings

2 Chronicles 24:17-21
2 Peter 1:16-end
Matthew 10:16-22

Opening prayer

God, who inspired Irenaeus to stand firm in the faith against wrong thinking and to keep the unity of the Church, grant that we may have a firm hold on our faith and work for the unity of all people: we ask this in the name of him who holds us in love, Jesus Christ our Lord.

Intercessions

Faithful and ever present God, as we praise you for the life of
Irenaeus, we pray for the people of France and especially of Lyons.
We give thanks for all who have shared their faith with us, and we
pray for all who seek to understand life and our purpose on the earth.
We ask your blessing upon all teachers and defenders of the faith,
and pray for all in theological colleges.

We remember all who are struggling with their faith, and those who have little faith in anything.
Lord, as you hold us in love,
help us to keep our hold on you.

Faithful and ever present God, we rejoice in the beauty and diversity of our world, and pray we may be aware of the sacredness of life in all beings.
We pray for areas of natural disasters such as flood or famine, and for all relief agencies.
We remember areas of the world spoiled by the greed or thoughtlessness of humans.
We ask your blessing upon all who are denied a fair living wage, or the essentials of a healthy life.
Lord, as you hold us in love,
help us to keep our hold on you.

Faithful and ever present God, we rejoice in your love and pray that it may be revealed in our dealings at home and in all we do.
We pray for homes where there is little or no love, and for all caught up in violent relationships.
We ask your blessing upon all children, that they may know they are loved and that their lives are precious.
We remember broken homes and children who have been taken into care.
Lord, as you hold us in love,
help us to keep our hold on you.

Faithful and ever present God, we rejoice in your compassion and pray for those who are lonely and feel unwanted.
We ask your blessing upon all who are fearful or anxious and who need a friend to help them.
We ask your blessing upon all who have been injured or who have been taken ill this week.
We pray for friends and loved ones who are suffering in any way (and in the silence we name them before you).
Lord, as you hold us in love,
help us to keep our hold on you.

Faithful and ever present God, we rejoice in the life and witness of Irenaeus and all your saints in glory.
We pray for those who have died this week, especially . . . (and in a time of stillness we pray for our loved ones departed).
Merciful Father,
accept these prayers for the sake of your Son, our Saviour, Jesus Christ.
Amen.

The peace

The deep peace of the Prince of Peace fill your hearts and minds, and be with you in all that you do.
The peace of the Lord be always with you.
And also with you.

Blessing

God's goodness guide you,
Christ's love lead you into light,
the Holy Spirit's power provide you with strength:
and the blessing of God Almighty, the Father, the Son and the Holy Spirit, be upon you and remain with you always.
Amen.

JULY

11 JULY

Benedict of Nursia

Benedict was born in about 480 in Nursia. He studied at Rome but left before completing his studies to become a hermit at Subacio. There he attracted disciples, whom he organised into twelve groups of ten. They lived semi-eremitical lives. In 525 there was an attempt by a dissatisfied faction to poison him. He left Subacio for Monte Cassino near Naples with a group of faithful followers. There he wrote the Rule for living a monastic life. Some of it was based on the traditional teaching of his predecessors but it was marked by a gentleness and moderation within the framework of obedience and authority. It also set out to give monks stability and encourage them not to wander from monastery to monastery. It was an orderly way of life based on a balance of liturgical prayer, sacred reading and manual work. Benedict was not a priest and did not intend to found a religious order. His achievement was to write the Rule which became a model for western monasticism. He died about the year 550.

Readings

Proverbs 2:1-9
1 Corinthians 3:10, 11
Luke 18:18-22

Opening prayer

Father, we offer you our thanks and praise for St Benedict, the father of western monasticism. Open our eyes to behold you, open our hearts to love you, give us minds to meditate upon you, and lives to proclaim you: we ask this in the name of Christ, our Saviour.

Intercessions

Lord of the loving heart, we give thanks for Benedict and the work of the Benedictine Order throughout the world.

We pray for the great monastery of Monte Cassino and all who spend time there.
We pray for all who have made a Rule of Life, that they may love and serve you in regular ways.
We ask your blessing upon the Church in Europe as it seeks to reveal your love and peace for all.
Lord most mighty,
hear us and help us.

Lord of the loving heart, we pray for the European Community as it strives to maintain unity and yet keep the diversity of nations.
We ask your blessing upon all who work to heal divisions and keep peace in our world; we remember the work of the United Nations.
We pray for areas where community life has broken down and people no longer communicate with one another.
We pray for our own land and for Elizabeth our Queen.
Lord most mighty,
hear us and help us.

Lord of the loving heart, we ask your blessing upon our homes and loved ones.
We pray for our communities and all who work within them.
We remember all who are without work and those suffering from debt or poverty.
We pray especially for people whose homes are being repossessed, or where there is violence and breakdown of family life.
Lord most mighty,
hear us and help us.

Lord of the loving heart, we pray for all who have lost contact with the world around them through dementia.
We ask your blessing upon their loved ones and carers.
We pray for all who are ill, injured or suffering from a disability.
In a time of silence we pray for those known to us who are in need . . .
Lord most mighty,
hear us and help us.

Lord of the loving heart,
Lord most mighty, we give you praise for Benedict and rejoice with all your saints in glory.

We pray for our loved ones departed (and in the stillness pray for them by name).
Merciful Father,
accept these prayers for the sake of your Son, our Saviour, Jesus Christ.
Amen.

The peace

The Lord of light and love,
the giver of life eternal,
enfold you in his presence and his peace.
The peace of the Lord be always with you.
And also with you.

Blessing

The joy of God the Creator,
the love of Christ the Saviour,
the guiding light of the Holy Spirit, go with you:
and the blessing of God Almighty, the Father, the Son and the Holy Spirit, be upon you and remain with you always.
Amen.

14 JULY

John Keble

John Keble was born at Fairford in 1792. He was the son of a priest and showed great skill as a poet while at Oxford University. He became a Fellow of Oriel College before being ordained deacon in 1816. After working in a parish for a while, he was elected as Professor of Poetry at Oxford in 1831. He was a leading light in the Oxford Movement, cooperating with Newman in writing a number of 'Tracts for the Times'. He then worked as a parish priest near Winchester. He wrote many hymns, including 'New every morning is the love' and 'Sun of my Soul, thou Saviour dear'. He died in 1866.

Readings

Lamentations 3:19-26
1 Corinthians 4:1-5
Matthew 5:1-8

Opening prayer

God our Creator, we give you praise and glory for the life and work of John Keble, and ask that we may be aware of your love towards us and all your creation, which comes to all that you have made, each and every day; we ask this in the love of Christ, our Saviour.

Intercessions

Lord of life, as we rejoice in John Keble's life, may we be aware of the newness of each morning and your unfailing love within it.
We ask your blessing upon the diocese of Winchester and all who live and work within it.
We pray for all who provide us with music, poetry and song, and ask your blessing this day upon hymn writers and organists.

We pray for the work of the Church amongst those who are seeking to protect and increase the beauty of the world.
Lord, we thy presence seek,
may ours this blessing be.

Lord of life, we give thanks for your presence within your creation, and pray that we may live in gentleness upon the earth.
We pray for all who strive to relieve suffering among oppressed and war-torn people.
We pray for the work of the Red Cross and for all working for peace and justice.
May we work for the goodness of all creation, its creatures and its resources.
Lord, we thy presence seek,
may ours this blessing be.

Lord of life, help us this and every day to live more nearly to you as we pray.
We pray for all who have brought love and purpose to our lives, asking your blessing upon our families and friends.
We pray for all who teach and those who inspire others by their goodness and grace.
We pray for all who live in squalid surroundings, those without teachers or examples of love and joy.
Lord, we thy presence seek,
may ours this blessing be.

Lord of life, watch by the sick, enrich the poor, with blessings from your boundless store.
We pray for all who are troubled in body, mind or spirit, and for those who are caring for them.
We remember any whose lives have suddenly fallen apart through some event or disaster.
We pray for friends and loved ones in their troubles (and in a time of silence name them before you, O God).
Lord, we thy presence seek,
may ours this blessing be.

Lord of life, as we give thanks for John Keble, we pray that we may also have a vision of the glory of your kingdom.
O Lord, in your dear love, fit us for perfect rest above.
We pray for all who are departed from us, remembering those who have died this week, and those whose memorial it is today . . .
We pray for our loved ones departed (in the silence of this moment).
Merciful Father,
accept these prayers for the sake of your Son, our Saviour, Jesus Christ.
Amen.

The peace

God help you this and every day
to live more nearly as you pray,
that you may abide in his love and peace.
The peace of the Lord be always with you.
And also with you.

Blessing

God give you a gentle heart towards all of creation,
a loving heart to all that you meet,
a warm heart in all your dealings,
a compassionate heart to the needy:
and the blessing of God Almighty, the Father, the Son and the Holy Spirit, be upon you and remain with you always.
Amen.

15 JULY

Swithun

Swithun was born in Wessex and educated in Winchester. He was chosen by King Egbert to be his chaplain and to teach his son Ethelwulf, who in 852 made him Bishop of Winchester. He was Bishop for ten years and was remembered for his works of charity and the building of churches. As he instructed, he was buried in a simple tomb outside the west door of the Old Minster. He is remembered today because of what happened after his death in 862. In the year 971 his body was translated into the new cathedral and placed in a shrine, which was going against his wishes. That day it rained extremely heavily. From this arose the legend that, if it rains on St Swithun's Day, it will rain for 40 days.

Readings

Proverbs 3:1-8
James 5:7-11, 13-18
Matthew 5:43-48

Opening prayer

Lord God, as we give thanks for the life and work of Swithun, give us a warm heart, a humble heart, a loving heart and a heart ever open to you, our Maker and Redeemer: we ask this in the name of Christ our Lord.

Intercessions

God our Creator, we give thanks for the work of Swithun in the building up of the Church in this land and we pray that we may help to build up your Church once more.
We pray for the diocese and Bishop of Winchester, for our own bishop, clergy and all who minister to us.

We ask that your Church may be an instrument of peace in a troubled world.
May your Church provide a shelter for the storm-tossed, the fearful and those whose lives are endangered.
In the seasons and storms of life,
be our strength and shield.

God our Creator, we remember those who have suffered from storms and floods.
We pray for those who have lost their livelihood, their homes or their loved ones.
We pray for areas where there is unrest, violence and war.
We ask your blessing upon all who have had to flee their homeland to survive, and we remember all who are refugees.
In the seasons and storms of life,
be our strength and shield.

God our Creator, we give thanks for all you have given to us, and ask your blessing upon our homes and our loved ones.
We pray for homes where the relationships are stormy and the home is in upheaval.
We pray for any who suffer through violent relationships.
We ask your blessing upon all who work to bring peace, healing and wellbeing to our communities.
In the seasons and storms of life,
be our strength and shield.

God our Creator, we remember all who have suddenly lost strength, health or the ability to cope with life.
We pray for all who are struggling with their own demons and fears.
We pray for those who have lost confidence in themselves or in others.
We pray for all who are troubled in any way (and in the silence pray for those we know).
In the seasons and storms of life,
be our strength and shield.

God our Creator, we give thanks for Swithun and pray that we may walk humbly upon the earth and live to your glory.

When the last great storm has passed may we find our rest and peace in you.
We pray for all who are departed this life (and in the time of stillness bring before God those whom we love but see no longer).
Merciful Father,
accept these prayers for the sake of your Son, our Saviour, Jesus Christ. Amen.

The peace

Seek justice and walk in integrity,
live in peace wherever you are
and walk humbly before your God.
The peace of the Lord be always with you.
And also with you.

Blessing

May you find in God
a shelter from the storms of life,
strength to face what lies ahead,
a delight in being alive:
and the blessing of God Almighty, the Father, the Son and the Holy Spirit, be upon you and remain with you always.
Amen.

19 JULY

Gregory, Bishop of Nyssa, and his sister Macrina

Gregory was the youngest brother of St Basil the Great. He was born in Caesarea in Cappadocia, in what is now Turkey, about the year 330. He was introduced to the faith by his older sister Macrina who had a strong influence on him throughout his life. It was Macrina who converted their household into a sort of monastery after the death of their father. Gregory was educated at Athens. In about 362 he was priested and in 371 consecrated as the Bishop of Nyssa. When his brother Basil and his sister Macrina died in the year 379, Gregory was deeply affected, but out of this trouble emerged a strong faith. He spent a lot of his skills in defending the Church against the Arian heretics. He is remembered as one of the great spiritual writers of the early Church. He died in the year 394. Gregory taught that God is not an object to be understood, but a mystery to be enjoyed.

Readings

Wisdom 9:13-17
1 Corinthians 2:9-13
John 16:12-15

Opening prayer

Lord of love, we give thanks for the family life of Macrina and Gregory. May we know you are present in our homes and be aware of your love and power to strengthen and guide us that we may live to your praise and glory: we ask this in the love of our Saviour, Jesus Christ.

Intercessions

Holy God, we ask your blessing upon the people of Turkey and the Christians within that country as a minority.

We pray for all who are facing difficulties or danger because of their faith.
We remember Christians trying to show your love and forgiveness in areas of hatred and prejudice.
We ask your blessing upon the Church throughout the world, as it seeks to reveal your love for all of creation.
Lord, in your grace and goodness,
hear and help us.

Holy God, we pray for all who walk gently upon the earth, and seek to conserve and protect endangered people or species.
We pray for minority groups and indigenous peoples who feel threatened or who are being forced to move.
We pray for all who work to protect the rights and the liberty of oppressed peoples.
We give thanks for the freedom we have and pray that we may use it to the good of others.
Lord, in your grace and goodness,
hear and help us.

Holy God, we give thanks for our homes and our friends.
May we be at home with you in our homes,
there revealing your light and love and abiding in your peace.
We ask your blessing upon all who enrich the lives of others by their own loving care and example.
We pray for all who do not have a loving home or a stable environment.
Lord, in your grace and goodness,
hear and help us.

Holy God, we remember all who suffer through the carelessness, prejudice or greed of others.
We pray for communities that hold old grievances, that they may find forgiveness and reconciliation.
We ask your blessing upon all healers of divisions and peacemakers.
We pray for all who are ill, and for those caring for them (in a moment of stillness we name those we know before God).
Lord, in your grace and goodness,
hear and help us.

Holy God, we give you praise and thanks for the family of Basil, Gregory and Macrina and their witness to the faith.
We pray for your saints and all the faithful departed (and in the quiet, bring before God those we want to remember).
Merciful Father,
accept these prayers for the sake of your Son, our Saviour, Jesus Christ.
Amen.

The peace

Trust in the Lord,
with all your heart and mind,
and let his presence fill you with peace and joy.
The peace of the Lord be always with you.
And also with you.

Blessing

The holy and ever present God
go with you and guide you,
be your strength and your joy:
and the blessing of God Almighty, the Father, the Son and the Holy Spirit, be upon you and remain with you always.
Amen.

26 JULY

Anna and Joachim

By a second-century tradition, the names given to the parents of the Virgin Mary are Anna and Joachim and so these are the grandparents of Jesus. This reminds us that Jesus was born into an earthly family with all its relationships and a lineage of people without one of whom, whether they were counted good or bad, Jesus could not have been born of Mary.

Readings

Zephaniah 3:14-18a
Romans 8:28-30
Matthew 13:16-17

Opening prayer

Father of all, who gave to Anna and Joachim a daughter who was to become the mother of our Lord, we give you thanks for their loving care and preparing Mary to be aware of you and open to your presence, and we ask you to guide us in our care for one another and especially for the young: we ask this in the name of him who was born into an earthly family, Jesus Christ, our Lord.

Intercessions

Loving Father, we give thanks for the Blessed Virgin Mary and for her parents, Joachim and Anna.
We pray that the Church may be a place of safety and nurture of young people, that they may grow in awareness of you in the mystery of life.
We remember those who taught us the faith and pray we may hand it on to the next generation.

We ask your blessing upon all who minister, preach and celebrate the sacraments, and show pastoral care for others; may we all share in this ministry.
Lord of our homes and our hearts,
be our hope and our joy.

Loving Father, we give thanks for our country and all who have worked to make it a place of freedom and peace.
We pray for Palestine and Jerusalem, that there may be peace within the diverse communities.
We pray for all who are involved in providing produce throughout the world, that they may receive fair trading and all may get a living wage.
We remember all who are without proper housing and food.
Lord of our homes and our hearts,
be our hope and our joy.

Loving Father, we give thanks for our ancestors, for without them we would not be here.
We remember our parents and grandparents with gratitude, and pray we may hand on care and goodness to all we live among.
We pray for those who are caring for the elderly at home or those in places of care.
We pray for those who see to the health and wellbeing of our communities.
Lord of our homes and our hearts,
be our hope and our joy.

Loving Father, we pray for those who reach out in love and care for others, for our local hospitals and medical staff.
We pray for the work of Age UK.
We pray for anyone who has been injured or hurt this week, for all who have fallen ill, and those who can no longer cope on their own.
We ask God's blessing upon all who are known to us and who are suffering in any way . . .
Lord of our homes and our hearts,
be our hope and our joy.

Loving Father, we give thanks for the Blessed Virgin Mary and her parents Joachim and Anna.
We ask your blessing upon members of our own families who are departed from us: (we pray for them and any others we want to name in the silence).
Merciful Father,
accept these prayers for the sake of your Son, our Saviour, Jesus Christ.
Amen.

The peace

The peace of God be in your hearts,
his peace in your home,
and in all your relationships.
The peace of the Lord be always with you.
And also with you.

Blessing

The love of God be upon you and your loved ones,
the presence of God keep you from harm,
the grace of God guide you into ways of peace:
and the blessing of God Almighty, the Father, the Son and the Holy Spirit, be upon you and remain with you always.
Amen.

29 JULY

Mary, Martha and Lazarus

We celebrate two sisters and their brother from Bethany at whose home Jesus received hospitality. Luke 10:38 tells how Jesus visited them. Martha who welcomed him to her home was distracted by the task of caring for him, whilst Mary sat at his feet. Martha became a symbol of the active life in God's service and Mary of the contemplative life. In the account from St John's Gospel, John 11:1-46, Jesus was sent for when Lazarus was taken ill. John tells us that Mary was the woman who anointed Jesus with her perfume, wet his feet with her tears, and wiped them dry with her hair. Jesus delayed and Lazarus died. When he came, Lazarus had been in the tomb for four days. Both sisters declared that, if he had been there, their brother would not have died (John 11:21, 32). His response to Martha was to say: 'I am the resurrection and the life.' She confessed him as the Christ, the Son of God. Jesus joined in the sisters' sorrow and wept with them. He then had the tomb opened and called Lazarus out.

Readings

Isaiah 25:6-9
Hebrews 2:10-15
John 12:1-8

Opening prayer

God our Father, as Christ was welcomed at the home of Mary, Martha and Lazarus with love, we pray that our home may be always open to you and that you may abide with us and in us: we ask this in the name of our Lord who came to dwell among us.

Intercessions

Lord, as you have called us into life, to know you and to love you, make us worthy of our calling.
Lord, teach us to abide in you and to know you always abide in us.

We ask your blessing upon all religious communities and houses that provide the stillness and peace to know you.
We pray for all who are unaware of your presence and love, and those who are out of touch through their busyness.
Lord, hear our prayer,
abide with us and help us.

Lord, we ask your blessing upon all who work to provide hospitality and comfort for others: we pray for all hotels, bed and breakfasts, and hostelries.
We ask your blessing upon all who reach out to make strangers and the lonely welcome.
We pray for all homeless people, for the street children of our world, and all those whose lives are endangered.
We remember all who work in the social services and all other carers.
Lord, hear our prayer,
abide with us and help us.

Lord, you bless our homes with your presence; may we welcome you each day and put our trust in you.
May our homes be places of welcome, peace and refreshment to all who come to visit us.
We ask your blessing upon all who feel left out and lonely within our society and may we be of help where we can.
We pray for young people who have left home, that they may find places of safety to live in.
Lord, hear our prayer,
abide with us and help us.

Lord, we remember all who have lost homes and loved ones through war or violence.
We pray for people forced off their land and who are without possessions or a homeland.
We remember all who are away from home due to illness, all in hospital or places of care.
We pray for friends and loved ones who are suffering in any way (and in a time of stillness name them before God).
Lord, hear our prayer,
abide with us and help us.

Lord, we give thanks for the home of Mary, Martha and Lazarus and the welcome they gave you.
We ask your blessing upon our loved ones departed and pray that they may be at home with you.
Merciful Father,
accept these prayers for the sake of your Son, our Saviour, Jesus Christ. Amen.

The peace

Abide in God and let God abide in you.
Abide in his light and love.
Abide in his power and peace.
The peace of the Lord be always with you.
And also with you.

Blessing

The light of God the Creator enfold you,
the love of Christ the Saviour surround you,
the leading of the Holy Spirit guide you.
Abide in God and let God abide in you:
and the blessing of God Almighty, the Father, the Son and the Holy Spirit, be upon you and remain with you always.
Amen.

30 JULY

William Wilberforce

William Wilberforce was born in Hull in 1759. He was educated at St John's College, Cambridge. He was a member of the evangelical group within the Church of England. His calling was to politics rather than ordination. He was made the MP for Hull at the age of 21 and later the MP for Yorkshire. He served in government throughout his life. He supported missionary outreach within the Church of England, and helped to found the Bible Society. Living in Clapham, London, he became the leader of the 'Clapham Sect' working for evangelical reforms within the Church of England. Today he is remembered most for his stand against the slave trade. After years of hard work, he saw the slave trade made illegal throughout the British Empire. He lived to see the abolition of slavery just before his death in 1833. We remember also today the work of Olaudah Equiano who died in 1797 and Thomas Clarkson who died in 1846, as they also campaigned for the trade in slaves to cease.

Readings

Job 31:16-23
Galatians 3:26-end; 4:6, 7
Luke 4:16-21

Opening prayer

Father, we give you thanks and praise for all who worked to end the slave trade. We remember today William Wilberforce, who as a Member of Parliament, sought to show God's compassion as he campaigned to abolish slavery. May we also show our compassion for all who are still ignored and ill-used and need our help: we ask this in the name of him who died to set us free, Jesus Christ our Lord.

Intercessions

Loving Lord, we give thanks for William Wilberforce and his vision that all people should be free and treated with respect.
We pray for the work of the Bible Society as it proclaims the Good News of your love.
We ask your blessing upon the Bishop of Hull, the diocese of York and all who live within that area.
Lord, we pray for your guidance upon the outreach of the Church and its care for the poor.
God, whose service is perfect freedom,
in your love, hear our prayer.

Loving Lord, we pray for all Members of Parliament that they may work with integrity and compassion.
We ask your blessing upon all who are still used as cheap labour and forced to work for low wages.
We ask your blessing upon all those whose human rights are ignored.
We pray that all our farmers and food producers may get a fair deal for their goods.
God, whose service is perfect freedom,
in your love, hear our prayer.

Loving Lord, we give thanks for the freedom of our land and all who work to protect it.
We remember all who are out of work and cannot find new employment.
We pray for those in sub-standard homes and poor conditions.
We pray for our homes and our loved ones and for their wellbeing.
God, whose service is perfect freedom,
in your love, hear our prayer.

Loving Lord, we remember all street children, and those who are encouraged to beg or steal for the gain of someone else.
We pray for the Children's Society and the Save the Children Fund.
We pray for all who are hindered by a disability or chronic illness.
We remember friends and loved ones who are ill (and in the stillness name them before God).
God, whose service is perfect freedom,
in your love, hear our prayer.

Loving Lord, we give thanks for life which is eternal.
We remember before you our friends and loved ones departed . . .
Merciful Father,
accept these prayers for the sake of your Son, our Saviour, Jesus Christ.
Amen.

The peace

God's peace in your hearts,
God's peace in your minds,
God's peace in all your activities,
God's peace in your rest:
The peace of the Lord be always with you.
And also with you.

Blessing

The Lord God be your strength,
lead you into the fullness of life,
and the glorious freedom of the children of God:
and the blessing of God Almighty, the Father, the Son and the Holy Spirit, be upon you and remain with you always.
Amen.

31 JULY

Ignatius Loyola

Ignatius, the youngest of eleven children, was born of a Basque noble family in 1491. He was brought up to be a soldier. In fighting against the French, he was wounded in 1521. His leg was broken and then was badly set: it had to be broken again and reset, and left him with a permanent limp. During his convalescence he wanted to read of deeds of valour. But the books available to him were a Life of Christ and Legends of the Saints. Due to this, he went through a conversion experience and lived for a year spending much of his time in prayer and penance at Manresa near the famous Montserrat monastery. He wrote his first draft of the *Spiritual Exercises*, some of which were in the tradition of Montserrat teaching. He set out on pilgrimage to Jerusalem. While he was there, some Franciscans persuaded him to return to Spain. He then studied at Barcelona, Alcala and Salamanca, finally gaining a Master of Arts degree in Paris in 1534. He lived an austere life and, though not ordained, gave spiritual direction to troubled people. In Paris he gathered around him a group of disciples to whom he gave the *Spiritual Exercises*: together they took vows of poverty, chastity and service to the Church. A small group of them set off for the Holy Land but at Venice found their way was barred. They then resolved to go to Rome and seek to become a religious order: by now they had all been ordained priest. They received papal approval and added the vow to go wherever the Pope sent them. Ignatius became their first Superior General. For the rest of his life he remained in Rome and directed the Society of Jesus. He died suddenly in 1556 but by then the work of the Jesuits had spread around the globe. They had reached England in 1542. Ignatius was canonised in 1622, and was acknowledged as a patron saint of spiritual exercises.

Readings

1 Kings 19:1-18
1 Corinthians 10:31–11:1
Luke 14:25-33

Opening prayer

God, who called Ignatius Loyola to reveal your glory in work and in action, grant that we also may glorify you not only in worship but in our work and in our daily lives. May we do all things to your glory through the help of him who revealed your glory among us, Jesus Christ, our Lord.

Intercessions

God of glory, we give thanks for the conversion of Ignatius Loyola, and his dedicating his life to your service: may we follow his example and live to your glory.
We pray for the Society of Jesus, and the work of the Jesuits throughout the world.
We pray for all who go on retreat, for those who conduct Ignatian retreats and teach his ways of meditation.
Lord, may we spend more time alone with you in stillness and prayer.
Lord, hear us,
and help us to live to your glory.

God of glory, we remember all who have been injured through war or violence, praying they may find a new peace in their lives.
We ask your blessing upon all who work for peace and unity in our world.
We pray for the work of the United Nations and for those who make decisions on the protecting of our world and its species.
Lord, grant us an awareness of you in, and your compassion for, all people.
Lord, hear us,
and help us to live to your glory.

God of glory, fill us with your light that we may reflect your glory in our homes and in all we do.
We ask your blessing upon all who work to make us aware of the beauty and mystery of your creation.
We pray for those who work to provide communities with places of rest, recreation and refreshment.
We remember before you our homes and our loved ones . . .
Lord, hear us,
and help us to live to your glory.

God of glory, we ask your blessing upon all who walk in darkness and despair that they may get a glimpse of your light and glory.
We pray for all who are ill at home, in hospital and those taken into care.
We pray for all who await surgery or a doctor's diagnosis.
We pray for friends and loved ones who are ill or in need at this time (and in the stillness name them before God).
Lord, hear us,
and help us to live to your glory.

God of glory, we give thanks for Ignatius Loyola and all who have lived and worked to reveal your glory.
We pray for all those departed from us (and in the silence bring before God any dear to us).
Merciful Father,
accept these prayers for the sake of your Son, our Saviour, Jesus Christ.
Amen.

The peace

Give glory to God in all that you do,
live in peace with all,
and seek to do God's will.
The peace of the Lord be always with you.
And also with you.

Blessing

God's glory be all about you,
God's grace go with you,
God's goodness guide you:
and the blessing of God Almighty, the Father, the Son and the Holy Spirit, be upon you and remain with you always.
Amen.

AUGUST

5 AUGUST

Oswald of Northumbria

Oswald was born about 605, the son of Ethelfrith of Northumbria. When he was only six, his father was killed in a battle against Edwin, Oswald, his older brothers and sister Ebba had to flee for safety. They ended up on the west coast of Scotland and Oswald came under the influence of the monks of Iona, where he was baptised. When Edwin died, two of his older brothers came with an army to claim their kingdom. However, they were both killed by the British king Cadwalla. In 634 Oswald came to Northumbria with a war band. The night before battle Oswald caused a cross to be made and held it while it was fixed in the ground; he and his soldiers prayed around it. They defeated and killed Cadwalla, and Oswald took over the kingdom. He united the northern kingdom, Bernicia, and the southern, Deira, into one. He sent to Iona for monks to come to Northumbria to teach the faith in his kingdom. Oswald often helped Aidan by acting as his interpreter among his own people. Oswald spent time in prayer, seated with his hands on his knees; he also gave to the poor. Sadly, his reign was short: he died in battle against the pagan Penda of Mercia at the battle of Maserfield in 642.

Readings

Wisdom 4:10-15
1 Peter 4:12-end
John 16:29-end

Opening prayer

We give thanks for the life and faith of Oswald, king of Northumbria, for his support of Christian mission, his generosity towards the poor and his own life of prayer. May we share in the outreach of the Church, its care for the poor and its witness of prayer: we ask this in the name of Christ, our Lord.

Intercessions

God our Creator, as we give thanks for St Oswald, we pray for the church in Bamburgh and at Heavenfield in Northumberland.
We pray for all who are called to defend their faith against a rising tide of unbelief.
We remember those who suffer for their faith, losing friends, homes, work and sometimes their lives.
May we not take our faith for granted, but grow strong in our love for God.
God, Holy and Strong One,
we put our trust in you.

God our Creator, we pray for leaders of nations who are striving to keep unity and peace.
We ask your blessing upon all who stand against terrorism and acts of violence.
We pray that we, who have richly received, may be generous towards others.
We remember nations and people impoverished through disasters and war.
God, Holy and Strong One,
we put our trust in you.

God our Creator, we give thanks for all who work to protect our freedom and ask your blessing upon them.
We pray for the communities to which we belong, that all may live in harmony and peace.
We pray for those who are new to our area, that they may find a welcome and a friendly care.
We ask your blessing upon our homes, our loved ones and our neighbours.
God, Holy and Strong One,
we put our trust in you.

God our Creator, we ask your blessing upon all who are deprived of their rights.
We pray for those who are distressed and disturbed by the way of life around them.
We pray for those who are not at peace with themselves or their

neighbours.
We remember all ill and suffering people (and in the stillness bring our concerns before God).
God, Holy and Strong One,
we put our trust in you.

God our Creator, we give thanks for St Oswald and all who have died in the faith.
We remember before you, O Lord, friends and loved ones departed . . .
Merciful Father,
accept these prayers for the sake of your Son, our Saviour, Jesus Christ. Amen.

The peace

The Light of God shine upon you,
and guide you in the ways of peace.
The peace of the Lord be always with you.
And also with you.

Blessing

God, the Father, keep you in his loving care,
Christ protect you in all your journeying,
the Holy Spirit be your guide in all that you do:
and the blessing of God Almighty, the Father, the Son and the Holy Spirit, be upon you and remain with you always.
Amen.

8 AUGUST

Dominic

Dominic was born about the year 1170, the youngest of four children of the Guzman family at Caleruega in Spain. He was educated by his uncle, the archpriest of Gamiel 'd Izan. He then joined the Austin Canons to live a life of prayer and penitence. In 1201 he became the Prior. In the year 1206 he went to Langedoc in France to help the Church to stand against the heretical sect of the Cathars. While at Toulouse he founded the Order of Preachers, the Dominicans, to assist in the work against the Cathars. The Order got the approval of the Pope in 1216. It was soon a good instrument in many countries, having a large impact on the Church. Dominic died at Bologna in 1221.

Readings

Ecclesiasticus 39:1-10
1 Corinthians 2:1-10
Luke 9:57-62

Opening prayer

God of grace and glory, we give you thanks for the life, witness and dedication of Dominic and the Dominicans: as they sought to spread the gospel through word and example, may we seek to do the same and witness to your saving love. We ask this in the name of Jesus Christ, our Lord.

Intercessions

Holy God, we give you thanks for Dominic and his preaching.
We pray for all Dominicans and their influence for good on the Church.
We ask your blessing upon all who are called to preach the word, or teach the faith.

We remember all who witness by quiet example and spirit-filled lives, and pray we may be among them.
Lord, as you have called us,
give us the grace to work for you.

Holy God, we pray for all who work through the media and influence the way we think.
We pray for publishers of daily newspapers, journals, books and all who work on the World Wide Web.
We ask your blessing upon musicians, poets, artists and craftspeople.
We remember all who work to improve our world, and pray that we may be among them.
Lord, as you have called us,
give us the grace to work for you.

Holy God, we ask your blessing upon national and local leaders, and pray for Elizabeth our Queen.
We pray for all who provide us with places of rest and entertainment.
We pray for our homes, our families and our friends, for their wellbeing and peace.
We ask your blessing upon all who seek to bring beauty and joy to communities, and pray that we may be among them.
Lord, as you have called us,
give us the grace to work for you.

Holy God, we pray for all who are separated from loved ones through illness or circumstance.
We remember those who are unemployed and those who are homeless.
As we pray for all who are ill, we remember before you those known to us . . .
We pray for all who seek to ease the suffering or distress of peoples, and pray that we may be among them.
Lord, as you have called us,
give us the grace to work for you.

Holy God, we give thanks for Dominic and all who have stood firm in the faith.
We pray for those who have died this week, and for the bereaved.

We remember our loved ones departed and ask that they be at peace and in the fullness of eternal life . . .
Merciful Father,
accept these prayers for the sake of your Son, our Saviour, Jesus Christ.
Amen.

The peace

The Good Shepherd, in his love, enfold you,
guide you and lead you into the ways of peace.
The peace of the Lord be always with you.
And also with you.

Blessing

God the Creator be your strength,
Christ the Saviour deliver you from evil,
the Spirit of God empower you to live in peace:
and the blessing of God Almighty, the Father, the Son and the Holy Spirit, be upon you and remain with you always.
Amen.

9 AUGUST

Mary Sumner

Mary Elizabeth Heywood was born in 1828. In 1848 she married a young curate, George Henry Sumner, a nephew of Archbishop Sumner. In 1888 George Sumner would be consecrated as the Bishop of Guildford. George and Mary Sumner had three children. Mary had a vision of uniting mothers of all classes to help them bring up their children in the Christian faith. She called a meeting for this purpose in 1876 and it was then that the Mothers' Union was founded with the ideal of bringing children up in a Christian family and home. It began as a parochial organisation but it grew steadily until it was an international one. Mary died on this day in 1921.

Readings

Proverbs 31:10-end
Hebrews 13:1-5
Luke 10:38-end

Opening prayer

We remember with gratitude Mary Sumner, who saw the need to give mothers encouragement and support in bringing up their families in the Christian faith. May we in our time see that all children get an opportunity to know God, and may we share in this way of witness: we ask this in the love of Jesus Christ, our Lord.

Intercessions

Loving Lord, as we give thanks for Mary Sumner, we pray for the work of the Mothers' Union and Mary Sumner House.
We pray for all who bring children to be baptised, that they will be encouraged to bring them up in the faith.

We ask your blessing upon 'Children's Church', Sunday schools and confirmation classes, and pray that children may always be made welcome in worship.
We pray for all who teach Religious Education and those who teach in theological colleges.
Lord, in your love, hear us
and keep us in your peace.

Loving Lord, we pray for all who work to relieve the suffering of children, and pray for the Save the Children Fund, and the Children's Society.
We remember all who help marriages where there are difficulties, tensions or troubles.
We pray for single parents and the bringing up of their children.
We ask your blessing upon all children who have been taken into care.
Lord, in your love, hear us
and keep us in your peace.

Loving Lord, we give thanks for our homes, and especially for our mothers who spend so much time and energy in caring for the home.
We pray for homes where a parent is ill and unable to cope.
We remember children who are often struggling to help out at home.
We give thanks for our loved ones and ask your blessing upon them.
Lord, in your love, hear us
and keep us in your peace.

Loving Lord, we pray for children caught up in war or in violence.
We pray for children separated from their parents due to the unrest or troubles within their country; we remember especially abandoned children.
We pray for children who are ill, for children's wards and hospitals.
We remember friends and loved ones who are struggling in any way (and in the silence name them before God).
Lord, in your love, hear us
and keep us in your peace.

Loving Lord, we give thanks for the Blessed Virgin Mary and the earthly home of Jesus.
We give thanks for Mary Sumner and for her vision.

We pray for all those who are departed from us (and in the stillness remember those dear to us by name).
Merciful Father,
accept these prayers for the sake of your Son, our Saviour, Jesus Christ.
Amen.

The peace

The Lord enfold you in his love,
keep you under his protection,
and grant you his peace.
The peace of the Lord be always with you.
And also with you.

Blessing

The love of the Creator surround you,
the grace of the Saviour be about you,
the light of the Spirit be within you:
and the blessing of God Almighty, the Father, the Son and the Holy Spirit, be upon you and remain with you always.
Amen.

10 AUGUST

Laurence, Deacon of Rome

Laurence was one of the seven deacons who assisted Pope Sixtus II, and was martyred only a few days before him in the Valerian persecutions of the Church. His examiners insisted that he produced the church's treasures. He promptly gathered a crowd of poor people, saying: 'These are the treasures of the Church.' A later addition to the story of his life has him being put to death on a gridiron. He died in the year 258.

Readings

Isaiah 43:1-7
2 Corinthians 9:6-10
Matthew 10:16-22

Opening prayer

God of grace and glory, we remember the bravery of Laurence of Rome, who refused to give the Emperor's prefect the church's treasures and pointed out that the real treasure of the Church is its people. May we never lose sight of this and reach out to draw others to you and your love: we ask this in the name of Jesus Christ, our Lord.

Intercessions

God, giver of life, may we put into practice what Laurence portrayed and show where the real treasures of the Church lie: not in the collecting of goods but in the service of others: we ask this in the name of Jesus our Lord.
We ask your blessing upon the Church's work with the poor, the outcasts and the oppressed.
We pray for Christian Aid, CAFOD, and all relief agencies.

May we, wherever we can, help those who are in need, and reveal your compassion.
Your kingdom come,
in us as it is in heaven.

God, giver of life, we pray that major industries and multinationals will respect minorities, indigenous peoples, and the earth's resources.
We pray that employers may show concern for their workers and not just look to profit.
We ask your blessing upon all who are used as cheap labour and who are trapped in poverty.
We pray that we may not squander the resources of the earth or misuse them through greed.
Your kingdom come,
in us as it is in heaven.

God, giver of life, we thank you for all whom you have given to us and pray we may treasure relationships much more than possessions.
May we learn to live simply, that others may simply live, and that future generations may not find a depleted or polluted world.
We pray for our homes and our loved ones, that we may treasure each other.
We remember all who are without a home of their own, or are in homes where there is little love.
Your kingdom come,
in us as it is in heaven.

God, giver of life, we pray for all who have suffered through the tyranny and greed of others.
We pray for all impoverished communities, and those without basic resources.
We remember all who are ill or distressed, especially in lands where there is not easy access to medical aid.
We remember friends and loved ones in their need (and in the silence pray for them).
Your kingdom come,
in us as it is in heaven.

God, giver of life, we give thanks for Laurence and all who have witnessed to your love and compassion.
We pray for all the faithful departed and remember especially those dear to us . . .
Merciful Father,
accept these prayers for the sake of your Son, our Saviour, Jesus Christ.
Amen.

The peace

Put your trust in God,
rejoice in his presence,
abide in his love,
live in his peace.
The peace of the Lord be always with you.
And also with you.

Blessing

Tread gently upon the earth,
respect all of creation,
seek to live in unity and peace:
and the blessing of God Almighty, the Father, the Son and the Holy Spirit, be upon you and remain with you always.
Amen.

11 AUGUST

Clare of Assisi

Clare was born in about 1193 at Assisi. As a young woman, she was attracted by the life, joy and preaching of St Francis. She escaped from home to join him. Soon after, she went to learn of community life from the Benedictines. When she founded the Community of the Poor Clares, it was for them to live a contemplative life in simplicity and corporate poverty. They were given a house by St Francis next to the church of St Damiano for their convent. Amongst those who joined her were her mother and two sisters. All lived a life of extreme poverty and austerity but with a love for nature and with joy. She was the first woman to write a religious Rule for women. She led the community at Assisi for 40 years. After Francis died, she supported his early companions in their desire to remain faithful to his teaching. She also counselled many leaders within the Church. She died in the year 1253. Some of her last words were: 'Blessed be God for creating me.'

Readings

Song of Solomon 8:6, 7
Philippians 3:8-14
Matthew 19:27-29

Opening prayer

Father, as Christ your Son became poor for our sakes, we give you thanks and praise for Clare who turned away from riches to live simply and to follow you in her love for all. May we learn where our true priorities lie and seek to live to your glory: we ask this in the name of our Lord and Saviour, Jesus Christ.

Intercessions

God our Creator, as we give thanks for Francis and Clare, we ask your blessing upon the Franciscan Orders and the Poor Clares.

We pray for all who give wise counsel and spiritual advice to others, for all who teach of your love in creation.
May we give ourselves, our hearts and lives in your service and in the love and care of your whole world and its creatures.
We pray for the Church in its efforts to bring peace and healing to areas of discord and distress.
Blessed are you, Lord, for creating us.
May we live to your glory.

God our Creator, we pray for all who lead, that they may also be able to listen and accept the wisdom of others.
We pray for all in places of power, that they may show compassion and care for those in their charge.
We ask your blessing upon all who work in the social services in their works of love and care for those in need.
We give thanks for all that we have and pray we may use it to your glory and the help of others.
Blessed are you, Lord, for creating us.
May we live to your glory.

God our Creator, we give thanks for those who have shown us that to serve you is a love affair.
We ask your blessing upon our homes and our loved ones, and pray that we may give one another the attention and love we all need.
We remember homes where there is little love and where relationships are breaking down.
We pray for all who are suffering from broken relationships, broken promises and broken hearts.
Blessed are you, Lord, for creating us.
May we live to your glory.

God our Creator, we ask your blessing upon all who work in healing and care: amid all the tensions, may they never lose sight of the caring love people need.
We pray for all who work among impoverished people and the outcasts of society.
We remember all who are ill or distressed and those who care for them and share in their suffering.

We ask your blessing upon friends and loved ones in their needs . . .
Blessed are you, Lord, for creating us.
May we live to your glory.

God our Creator, we give you praise for Clare and Francis as they have revealed your love in their lives.
We remember our friends and loved ones departed (and in the stillness pray they may rejoice in the love of God).
Merciful Father,
accept these prayers for the sake of your Son, our Saviour, Jesus Christ. Amen.

The peace

God give you grace to grow in holiness,
to be generous to all,
and to live in peace.
The peace of the Lord be always with you.
And also with you.

Blessing

Live not to yourself alone,
reach out to others in love,
deal kindly with all,
and live to God's glory:
and the blessing of God Almighty, the Father, the Son and the Holy Spirit, be upon you and remain with you always.
Amen.

13 AUGUST

Jeremy Taylor

Jeremy Taylor was born at Cambridge in 1613. He was educated at Gonville and Caius College. He was ordained in 1633 and soon became a chaplain with the Royalists in the Civil War. He was captured and imprisoned for a short time. Once released, he went to Wales where the Earl of Carbery offered him a place of refuge. It was while there that he probably had the time to write *The Rule and Exercise of Holy Living* in 1650 and that of *Holy Dying* the following year. He left Wales in 1658 for Ireland to lecture there and two years later he was consecrated the Bishop of Down and Connor. Many of the clergy held to Presbyterian views, so ignored him, and the Roman Catholics rejected him as a Protestant. As a result, he treated both sides harshly. His health suffered through the stress of continuous conflicts and he died in 1667.

Readings

I Kings 3:6-10
2 Titus 7, 8, 11-14
Matthew 5:13-19

Opening prayer

Loving Lord, as we give thanks for Jeremy Taylor, may we seek to live to your glory in our work and in all that we do, and as you have called us to work with you, make us worthy of our calling: we ask this in the name of Jesus Christ, our Saviour.

Intercessions

Gracious God, we give you thanks for the life and writings of Jeremy Taylor. We ask your blessing upon the Church in Ireland and we pray for the people and diocese of Down and Connor.

We pray for our diocese, for its bishop . . . , its clergy and all who teach us the faith by word and example.
We pray for the Church throughout the world, that it may be an instrument of healing, love and revealing of your presence.
May we seek to live lives of dedication, service and love.
Lord of life, in your love,
hear us and help us.

Gracious God, we ask your blessing upon Elizabeth our Queen, our Parliament and all who are in positions of government.
We pray for all who are involved in world trade, that it may be done with integrity, and fair dealing.
We remember all who work for peace, unity and concord between peoples and nations, and pray for the work of the United Nations.
May we live in peace with ourselves, our loved ones and our neighbours, that peace in our area may grow.
Lord of life, in your love,
hear us and help us.

Gracious God, we ask that our homes may be where faith and love are given the chance to grow.
We pray for homes where there are young children, that they may be encouraged to enjoy life and to share their love.
We remember children and adults who feel rejected or unwanted, and pray their hurts may be healed and love restored.
We give thanks for loving homes and ask your blessing upon us and our loved ones.
Lord of life, in your love,
hear us and help us.

Gracious God, Lord of life, in your love, we remember all who are terminally ill at home, in a hospice, or place of care.
We pray for their friends and loved ones in their distress and shared suffering.
We ask your blessing upon all who are struggling with life and the difficulties around them.

We pray for friends and loved ones in need or in illness (and in the silence remember them by name).
Lord of life, in your love,
hear us and help us.

Gracious God, as we give thanks for Jeremy Taylor, may we live in a way that shows we love you and believe that, in you, life is eternal. We pray for all the faithful departed, and remember before you our loved ones departed . . .
Merciful Father,
accept these prayers for the sake of your Son, our Saviour, Jesus Christ. Amen.

The peace

Trust in the Lord with all your mind,
love the Lord with all your heart,
let the Lord guide you into his ways of peace.
The peace of the Lord be always with you.
And also with you.

Blessing

God the Creator be your strength,
Christ the Saviour surround you with love,
the Holy Spirit enfold you in peace:
and the blessing of God Almighty, the Father, the Son and the Holy Spirit, be upon you and remain with you always.
Amen.

20 AUGUST

Bernard of Clairvaux

Bernard was born about the year 1090 at Fontaines near Dijon, the third son of a Burgundian nobleman. He was educated by secular canons at Chatillon-sur-Seine. There he was known as a charming man, full of wit and eloquence. In 1112 with 21 companions, including some of his brothers, he went to the poverty-stricken Citeaux. This influx of new recruits probably saved it from extinction. After a few years, Bernard was made the Abbot at a new foundation at a place he called Clairvaux, the Valley of Light. Under acute poverty, he was initially too severe with his community. When he realised this, he gave up preaching for a while and saw to a better food supply. He built up the community with a great sense of leadership. Bernard was a powerful preacher, teacher, and organiser. In his own lifetime hundreds of other houses were founded on the Citeaux or Cistercian system, including Rievaulx, Fountains and Jervaulx in North Yorkshire, Whitland in Dyfed, Boxley in Kent and Mellifont in County Louth. Citeaux numbered 700 monks at Bernard's death in 1153. He was declared a Doctor of the Church in 1830; he is also known as 'the last of the Fathers'.

Readings

Ecclesiasticus 15:1-6
Revelation 19:5-9
John 17:20-26

Opening prayer

Holy God, who called Bernard, whose heart was on fire with love for you, to a life of dedication as a Cistercian, may the light of your presence and the fire of your love stir our hearts and set them ablaze with love for you: we ask this in the name of Christ our Lord.

Intercessions

Loving Lord, we give you praise for the life and example of Bernard, who led your Church in discipline and love, and encouraged all to walk as children of light.
Lord, may we and your whole Church burn with love for you, with love in our thinking, love in our speaking, love in our actions, and deep love for your world.
We pray for religious communities, and today especially for the Cistercians.
We ask your blessing upon all who proclaim your love for all of creation.
Lord of light and love,
hear us and guide us.

Loving Lord, we remember all who work in mountain rescue, relief agencies and the emergency services.
We pray for all who work to defend our lives from violence and evil.
We pray for all who are shepherds, for wool merchants, and providers of clothing.
We ask your blessing upon the world's poor, and pray that we may be of help where we can.
Lord of light and love,
hear us and guide us.

Loving Lord, we thank you for our homes, for all who love us, and for those who have enriched our lives.
As we have freely received, may we give freely and with generosity.
May we live lives that never lose sight of your love for us and your presence ever with us.
We pray for families where there is unrest or trouble and where there is a danger of breakdown.
Lord of light and love,
hear us and guide us.

Loving Lord, we pray for all who feel lost in the turmoil of life and for the lonely.
We remember all who find it difficult to make friends or to express their needs.

We pray for all who are separated from loved ones through illness.
We ask your blessing upon all who are ill or distressed in any way (and in the silence we pray for those whom we know).
Lord of light and love,
Hear us and guide us.

Loving Lord, we give thanks for Bernard and his example of a life burning with love: may he rejoice with all your saints in glory.
We pray for our loved ones departed . . . that they may rejoice in the love of God and life eternal.
Merciful Father,
accept these prayers for the sake of your Son, our Saviour, Jesus Christ.
Amen.

The peace

Let there be love in your speaking,
grace in your dealings,
generosity in your relationships,
and peace in your life.
The peace of the Lord be always with you.
And also with you.

Blessing

God, who created you out of love, is with you;
Christ, who redeemed you by his love, is with you;
the Holy Spirit, who sustains you with his love, is with you:
and the blessing of God Almighty, the Father, the Son and the Holy Spirit, be upon you and remain with you always.
Amen.

27 AUGUST

Monica

Monica was the mother of Augustine of Hippo, whose feast day follows hers. She was born in North Africa of a Christian family in 332. She married a pagan named Patricius, whom she converted to Christianity. They had three children of whom Augustine was the eldest. Augustine ascribes his conversion as due to the example of his mother and her prayers. He wrote, 'She never lets me out of her prayers that you, O God, might say to the widow's son, "Young man, I say to you, arise!"' Patricius died when Monica was 40. She expressed a desire to be buried beside him. Monica was overjoyed when Augustine was baptised. In 387, Monica, Augustine and his friends set out on a journey back to Africa. Monica died on the way at Ostia in Italy at the age of 55; both her sons were with her.

Readings

Ecclesiasticus 26:1-3,13-16
1 Peter 3:1-9
Luke 7:11-17

Opening prayer

Gracious God, we give you thanks and praise for the motherly love of Monica, who through her patience and prayer encouraged her son Augustine to be baptised and active as a Christian. Grant that we may, through gentle care and love, help others to come to know and love you: we ask this in the love of Christ, our Lord and Saviour.

Intercessions

Lord, giver of life, as we remember the prayer and patience of
Monica, we remember all who have helped us to grow in the faith.
We pray for all who are wavering in their faith or need help to know
your love and compassion.

We ask your blessing upon all who teach of your love by word or example; we pray for preachers, teachers and all who gently reveal your love.
We pray for those who teach children the faith and those who seek out the confused and lost to bring them to your love.
Lord, in your love,
hear, and strengthen us.

Lord, giver of life, we ask your blessing upon all who seek to bring peace and joy to the world.
We remember those who stand firm against evil practices and strive for fair dealing and justice for all people.
We pray for those who work in conservation and the preservation of endangered species.
May we treat the earth with care and love as it is your creation, O God.
Lord, in your love,
hear, and strengthen us.

Lord, giver of life, may we find ways of communicating your loving care in the way we live.
We pray for our homes and loved ones, that they all may become aware of the wonders of life and your love for all of creation.
We ask your blessing upon the communities in which we live, and pray that they may reveal your compassion and glory.
We remember those within our communities who are struggling and pray that we may be of some help.
Lord, in your love,
hear, and strengthen us.

Lord, giver of life, we remember all whose lives are full of darkness, doubt and despair, and pray that they may be brought into your light.
We remember all who suffer from clinical depression and pray they may find a new peace in you and your love.
We pray for all who are ill at home or in hospital, that they may find hope and strength in you.
We remember friends and loved ones who are ill (and pray for them in the stillness).
Lord, in your love,
hear, and strengthen us.

Lord, giver of life, we give you thanks for those who have prayed for us and supported us in the faith.
We give thanks for Monica and the faithful love of mothers.
We pray for our friends and loved ones departed . . .
Merciful Father,
accept these prayers for the sake of your Son, our Saviour, Jesus Christ.
Amen.

The peace

The Lord enfold you in love,
wrap you round with his presence,
clothe you with his peace.
The peace of the Lord be always with you.
And also with you.

Blessing

The power of God protect you,
the peace of God go with you,
the presence of God abide with you:
and the blessing of God Almighty, the Father, the Son and the Holy Spirit, be upon you and remain with you always.
Amen.

28 AUGUST

Augustine of Hippo

Augustine was born in Tagaste (Algeria) in 354 of a pagan father and Christian mother. Despite the guidance of his mother, Monica, he joined the Manichean sect, kept a concubine and had an illegitimate child. He was converted in 386 and baptised by Bishop Ambrose of Milan, who had greatly influenced him. He returned to Africa in 388 with some friends to live a monastic-style life. In 391 he was ordained priest, then coadjutor-bishop of Hippo in 395; the following year he became the Bishop of Hippo (now known as Annaba in Algeria). Augustine wrote and preached in defence of the faith. His intellectual brilliance, his wide education and his mystical insight combined to make him an amazing personality, and one of the most influential Doctors of the Church. Among his most famous writings are the *Confessions,* the sermons on the Gospel of St John, *De Trinitate* and, towards the end of his life, *De Civitate Dei.* He died in the year 430.

Readings

Ecclesiasticus 39:1-10
Romans 13:11-13
Matthew 23:8-12

Opening prayer

Loving Lord, as you called Augustine, may we hear your call in our restless hearts and troubled minds and so be drawn towards your presence, your peace and your power to renew and restore us: we ask this in the name of our Lord Jesus Christ.

Intercessions

Almighty God, you have made us for yourself and our hearts are restless till they rest in you; help us to discover you are the life of all who love you and the strength of those who serve you.

We ask your blessing upon those who are seeking for meaning and purpose in their lives, and pray that the Church may be able to help and guide them.
We pray for all who are training for ministry or to teach Religious Education, that their studies may be based on their awareness of you.
We remember those who quietly pray for and seek to help others on their journey of life.
May we rest in you,
and know your peace.

Almighty God, we bring before you our troubled world and the distress of nations.
We ask your blessing upon all caught up in war or acts of terrorism, and all who are made refugees.
We pray for the work of the United Nations and the peace-keeping forces of our world.
We pray that we all may learn to respect one another and all of your creation.
May we rest in you,
and know your peace.

Almighty God, we pray that our homes may be places of peace, of rest and refreshment.
We ask your blessing upon those who are restless and find it difficult to be still or at peace, remembering homes where there is deep unrest.
We pray for families that are deeply in debt and are finding it difficult to cope.
We remember those who teach us where true riches are to be found and not in forever needing more and more possessions.
We pray for the work of the Citizens Advice Bureau and the Samaritans.
May we rest in you,
and know your peace.

Almighty God, grant us in all perplexities your guidance, in all dangers your protection, and in all our sorrows your peace.
Lord, tend your sick ones, refresh your weary ones, and calm all suffering ones.

We remember in your presence those who are known to us and are ill or in need . . .
We ask your blessing upon those who work in rescue and healing and protection.
May we rest in you,
and know your peace.

Almighty God, as Augustine rose from his old ways to newness of life, we remember all who are departed from us and now walk in the newness of life in your glory.
We remember before you our friends and loved ones departed . . .
Merciful Father,
accept these prayers for the sake of your Son, our Saviour, Jesus Christ. Amen.

The peace

Trust in God,
abide in his love,
rest in his peace.
The peace of the Lord be always with you.
And also with you.

Blessing

The Lord is your light, your strength and your salvation: abide in him as he abides in you: and the blessing of God Almighty, the Father, the Son and the Holy Spirit, be upon you and remain with you always. **Amen.**

29 AUGUST

Beheading of John the Baptist

The Gospels relate how John the Baptist fearlessly opposed Herod Antipas's unlawful marriage to Herodias (Matthew 14:1-12, Mark 6:17-29). The outraged ruler had John imprisoned. In a rash moment he promised to give Salome whatever she desired that was within his power. Encouraged by her mother, she asked for the head of John the Baptist. Herod Antipas was trapped, for he feared to break a promise made in the presence of others. He had John's head brought to her. His disciples took his body and buried it. When Jesus heard of it, he took up John's call, preaching: 'The kingdom of heaven has come near.'

Readings

Jeremiah 1:4-10
Hebrews 11:32–12:2
Matthew 14:1-12

Opening prayer

Father, we give you thanks for the courage and vision of John the Baptist and for his being the herald of Christ. May we stand firm for freedom and truth, and help to draw others into awareness of you and your love: we ask this in the name of Christ, our Lord.

Intercessions

God of grace, as we give thanks for John the Baptist, we pray for all who stand up against injustice or tyranny.
We pray for the Church in areas where it is being persecuted or is under severe restrictions.
We remember Christians who have lost their work, their homes or their lives because they have spoken out.

Lord, may we be firm in our faith and stand against all that mars or despoils your world.
Lord, your kingdom come,
on earth as it is in heaven.

God of grace, we remember lives spoiled by hatred, greed or lawlessness.
We pray for those who work to protect the weak and vulnerable, often at the risk of their own lives.
We remember those who are suffering under intolerant regimes, through war or its aftermath.
We pray for Elizabeth our Queen, for all in positions of authority and all who are put in charge of others.
Lord, your kingdom come,
on earth as it is in heaven.

God of grace, we pray for families that are suffering through disaster or through violence.
We remember families torn apart, who are refugees, impoverished, with a loved one in prison, or suffering from great upheavals in society.
We pray for our homes, our loved ones and the communities to which we belong.
May we, where possible, be of help and guidance to any we encounter in need.
Lord, your kingdom come,
on earth as it is in heaven.

God of grace, we remember all who have laid down their lives for others; we pray for their families and friends in their loss.
We pray for those who suffer from areas of war or unrest.
We remember the countless people without proper medical care or attention, and we pray for those who work to relieve this situation.
We ask your blessing on all who are ill (and we pray for those known to us).
Lord, your kingdom come,
on earth as it is in heaven.

God of grace, we give thanks for John the Baptist and his witness, and we pray for any who have stood up for the truth and died this week. We remember our own loved ones and friends departed . . .
Merciful Father,
accept these prayers for the sake of your Son, our Saviour, Jesus Christ.
Amen.

The peace

Put your trust in God,
let his love fill you with joy and peace.
The peace of the Lord be always with you.
And also with you.

Blessing

Go out in the strength of the Almighty,
his help strengthen you,
his hand guide you,
his heart hold you:
and the blessing of God Almighty, the Father, the Son and the Holy Spirit, be upon you and remain with you always.
Amen.

30 AUGUST

John Bunyan

John Bunyan was born in 1628 of a poor family at Elstow in Bedfordshire; he probably acquired his knowledge and imagery and mastery of language from the Bible. He was introduced to some Protestant texts and thoughts by his wife who was a woman of piety. Bunyan suffered a great deal from the repressive measures of the Royalists after the Restoration and spent his time writing when he was in prison. His best known work is *The Pilgrim's Progress* which is concerned with the journey through life and the hazards that are met whilst looking towards salvation. He died on this day in 1688.

Readings

Tobit 8:4-7
Hebrews 12:1, 2
Luke 21:21, 34-36

Opening prayer

Almighty God, as we give thanks for the life of John Bunyan and for his writing *The Pilgrim's Progress,* we rejoice in your abounding grace and pray we may be aware of your presence and love in our journey on this earth: we ask this in the name of Jesus Christ, our Lord.

Intercessions

God of grace, as we remember John Bunyan, we ask that we may become aware that we are journeying in your kingdom and your presence.
We pray for all places that have been designated pilgrim or holy places; through them may we discover the holiness of life and of the earth itself.
We ask your blessing upon places of retreat and stillness, on places where meditation and prayer are taught.

We pray for all who go on pilgrimage, that they may discover they live in your presence and you are there in the journey of life.
Lord, hear us,
help us and guide us.

God of grace, we pray for all who strive to be valiant for truth, justice and freedom.
We pray that the legal systems may have integrity and care for each individual.
We pray for those working among the oppressed peoples and poor of our world.
We pray for Amnesty International and for their seeking to free the falsely accused.
We pray for all whose lives are limited, through despotic rule or harsh laws.
Lord, hear us,
help us and guide us.

God of grace, we give thanks for all that you have given us and pray that we may be generous and caring to any in need.
May we remember that, even if our contribution is small, it can be of help to those who are poor.
We pray for our homes and loved ones, for joy, peace and love between us.
We remember homes where there is conflict, violence or hatred, and pray for all in their suffering.
Lord, hear us,
help us and guide us.

God of grace, we ask your blessing upon those who are lost in the 'wilderness of this world'.
We pray for those sinking in the 'Slough of Despond' or whose lives are darkened by the 'Giant Despair'.
We pray for those caring for the deeply distressed and those who have lost hope.
We remember friends and loved ones in illness or beset by troubles: (and in the stillness pray for them) . . .
Lord, hear us,
help us and guide us.

God of grace, grant when our life's journey does cease, you will enfold us in your peace.
We pray for those who are now in the fullness of eternal life . . .
Merciful Father,
accept these prayers for the sake of your Son, our Saviour, Jesus Christ.
Amen.

The peace

The Lord God is your companion,
he travels with you and is within you,
find in him your rest and your peace.
The peace of the Lord be always with you.
And also with you.

Blessing

God of grace abounding
guide you through the journey of life,
be your light and love and your salvation:
and the blessing of God Almighty, the Father, the Son and the Holy Spirit, be upon you and remain with you always.
Amen.

31 AUGUST

Aidan of Lindisfarne

Aidan was an Irish monk who joined the community on Iona; from there he was sent at King Oswald's request to preach and teach in the kingdom of Northumbria. He was consecrated bishop, then given the island of Lindisfarne by King Oswald. Oswald, who had become a Christian while on Iona, assisted Aidan by being his interpreter. Aidan set up a monastery in the style of Iona, where he educated men to be priests, and sent them out in mission throughout England. His simple way of life, his care for the poor, his seeking to free those unjustly brought into slavery and his walking about preaching and praying with people won him popular support and many conversions. He was known to be a gentle man and a man of prayer. He was instrumental in giving Christianity a strong foothold beyond the boundaries of Northumbria. He died in Bamburgh in 651.

Readings

Isaiah 6:1-8
1 Corinthians 9:16-19
Matthew 23:8-12

Opening prayer

Holy God, we give you thanks and praise for the coming of Aidan to Lindisfarne and for his reaching out from there in mission. As we remember his gentleness, generosity and pastoral care, may we follow his example and walk gently upon the earth and seek to reveal your love for all of creation: we ask this in the love of Christ, our Lord.

Intercessions

Lord of love, we give thanks for Aidan who helped to spread the light of Christ in the Dark Ages: may the light of Christ shine in our lives.

We pray for the church on Lindisfarne in its caring for the local community and for the pilgrims.
As Aidan was a faithful teacher and pastor, we pray for all bishops, priests, deacons and teachers of the faith.
We pray for all involved in pastoral care, for social workers, medics, and those who are caring for neighbours.
Lord, as you sent Aidan, hear us,
strengthen us to go out and serve you.

Lord of love, as we give thanks for the generosity of Aidan and his community, and the freeing of slaves, we pray for those who stand against all forms of slavery and cheap labour.
We pray for all held through injustice, false accusations, or through despotism and tyranny.
We remember those who are slaves to drugs or vice or addicted in any way: we ask your blessing upon all who seek to help them.
We pray for migrant peoples, for those forced off their land, and for those who are homeless and refugees.
Lord, as you sent Aidan, hear us,
strengthen us to go out and serve you.

Lord of love, we pray that our homes may be places of gentleness and patience.
We ask your blessing upon young people and the challenges and difficulties they are facing: and we pray for all seeking to guide them.
We pray for those who are generous with their talents and time within the community.
We remember the housebound and the lonely, and those who seek to help them.
Lord, as you sent Aidan, hear us,
strengthen us to go out and serve you.

Lord of love, we pray for all whose lives are darkened by fear, anxiety or a lack of love.
We remember all who are confused by the pace of life or by what is happening in the world.
We pray for all who are caught up in the unrest of nations and are fearful for their future.

We pray for those who are ill (and remember before God those known to us).
Lord, as you sent Aidan, hear us,
strengthen us to go out and serve you.

Lord of love, we give thanks for Aidan and the saints of Lindisfarne.
We pray for all who have inspired us and are now departed from us (we remember them and our loved ones departed . . .).
Merciful Father,
accept these prayers for the sake of your Son, our Saviour, Jesus Christ.
Amen.

The peace

Walk gently upon the earth,
be generous to all,
and seek to share God's peace.
The peace of the Lord be always with you.
And also with you.

Blessing

Our glorious God give you grace to proclaim the Good News in word and deed, to live in love and peace, and respect for all creation: and the blessing of God Almighty, the Father, the Son and the Holy Spirit, be upon you and remain with you always.
Amen.

SEPTEMBER

3 SEPTEMBER

Gregory the Great

Gregory was born in 540, the son of a Roman Senator. He served as a magistrate and was made Prefect of Rome in 573. When his father died, he resigned his office, sold his inheritance and became a monk. In 579 he was sent to Constantinople as papal legate to the Patriarch. He returned to Rome in 586 and was elected Pope in 590. Gregory proved to be a great administrator and diplomat. He tightened church discipline and liturgical practice and reorganised the lands belonging to the Holy See. He initiated the mission to England, sending Augustine and 40 monks from his own monastery to convert the people of Kent. Due to his theological and pastoral writings, he has the title 'Doctor of the Church'. His spirituality was based on a deep love and desire for God and he is sometimes given the title 'Doctor of Desire'. As the Pope, he was the first to style himself 'Servant of the servants of God'. He died in 604.

Readings

Ecclesiasticus 47:8-11
1 Thessalonians 2:3-8
Luke 22:24-30

Opening prayer

God most mighty, we give you thanks for St Gregory and his mission to re-evangelise England. May we face the new challenges of mission, outreach, and church reform with the love of you in our hearts and all our actions: we ask this in the name of Christ our Lord.

Intercessions

We rejoice in the mission instigated by Pope Gregory and his sending of Augustine and Mellitus and the monks to England.

We pray for St Peter's, Rome, for Canterbury Cathedral, and for St Paul's, London: for all who serve there and those who live within their areas.
We ask your blessing upon all who are involved in mission and the building up of the faith in this land.
We pray for those who are ordained bishop, priest or deacon, that they may be servants of the servants of God.
God of grace and glory,
hear our prayer.

We ask your blessing upon London and Canterbury and all our cities in these times of tension and transition in our cities.
We ask your blessing upon Elizabeth our Queen, the royal family, the Houses of Parliament and all who work there.
We pray for all who work for unity and peace in our world.
We ask your blessing upon all areas of our world where there is tension, terror or tyranny.
God of grace and glory,
hear our prayer.

We give thanks for our homes and our loved ones and ask your blessing upon them.
We pray for all young people in their places of learning, and remember schools that are overcrowded or have difficulty in staffing.
We pray for all who have learning difficulties, and for the teams of people who come to help them.
We ask your blessing upon the communities to which we belong and upon those who sustain them and enrich them by their talents.
God of grace and glory,
hear our prayer.

We pray for those who work in the National Health Service and ask your blessing upon all doctors and nurses as they serve the community.
We pray for those who are in hospital, especially those awaiting operations or tests for their illness.
We pray for friends and loved ones who are ill or troubled in any way.
We remember before you, O God, those who are known to us: we pray for them and for our own wellbeing . . .
God of grace and glory,
hear our prayer.

We give thanks for the life and talents of Pope Gregory and for all your saints in glory.
We pray for the faithful departed, and name before you, O God, those dear to us . . .
May they rejoice in your peace and rest in your glory.
Merciful Father,
accept these prayers for the sake of your Son, our Saviour, Jesus Christ. Amen.

The peace

Trust in the Lord with all your heart and all your mind,
let his love fill you with joy and peace,
and empower you to live to his glory.
The peace of the Lord be always with you.
And also with you.

Blessing

The glory of God go with you,
the grace of Christ guide you,
the goodness of the Holy Spirit fill you:
and the blessing of God Almighty, the Father, the Son and the Holy Spirit, be upon you and remain with you always.
Amen.

4 SEPTEMBER

St Cuthbert

(See 20 March)

13 SEPTEMBER

John Chrysostom

John was born in Antioch about the year 347. He trained as an orator and lawyer. He became a monk c.373, then a priest in 386. He soon became famous as a brilliant preacher; this gained him the name Chrysostom or 'the golden-mouthed'. Against his wishes, he was made the Patriarch of Constantinople in 398. There he faced much opposition in his desire for reforms of the court and the clergy. He fell foul of the Empress Eudoxia and was sent into exile. After an earthquake he was recalled. He resumed his reforms and plain speaking and once again was sent into exile. He died of exhaustion and starvation in 407. He is honoured as one of the four Greek Doctors of the Church.

Readings

Jeremiah 1:4-10
Ephesians 3:8-12
Matthew 5:13-19

Opening prayer

God of grace and goodness, we thank you for the gifts of eloquence in his teaching and patience in his sufferings that you gave to John Chrysostom and that he remained faithful in love for you and your power to save. May we be strengthened through his example and be strong in our love for and faith in you: we ask this in the name of Christ, our Saviour.

Intercessions

O God our Creator, our life and our talents come from you; may we use them to your praise and glory.

We give thanks that John Chrysostom was a gifted preacher and stood out against the evils of his time; may we also have the strength to stand for goodness and truth.
May your Church witness to your love of all creation and your compassion towards all people.
We ask your blessing upon the Orthodox Church, the Patriarch of Constantinople and all who are standing firm in their faith against persecution.
God, our strength,
our hope is in you.

O God our Creator, may the leaders of Parliament and industry be strong enough to stand against corruption and greed.
We pray that all developers and industrialists may respect the earth and its limited resources, and care for the planet.
We remember all who work in conservation and pray especially for those whose lives are at risk.
We ask your blessing upon those who give their lives in the service of others.
God, our strength,
our hope is in you.

O God our Creator, we give thanks for those who have been an example to us, and pray that we may be the same to others.
We remember those who sought to show us the beauty and the fragility of the earth, and pray that we may see the preciousness and uniqueness of all things.
May we learn to live without the desire to forever possess more and more and to walk gently upon the earth.
We ask your blessing upon our homes and our loved ones.
God, our strength,
our hope is in you.

O God our Creator, we pray for all who have been exiled from land or homes or whose land is war-torn or exhausted.
We pray for all who are suffering from encroaching deserts and who live in poverty and hunger.
We ask your blessing upon all who work to relieve suffering of any form.

We pray for friends and loved ones who are ill or in need . . .
God, our strength,
our hope is in you.

O God our Creator, in you alone is life which is eternal.
We praise you for John Chrysostom and all who have died defending their faith.
We pray for families recently bereaved and that their loved ones departed may be in your peace.
We remember our own loved ones who have died and pray they may rejoice in your gift of life eternal.
Merciful Father,
accept these prayers for the sake of your Son, our Saviour, Jesus Christ.
Amen.

The peace

The Lord is your life and love,
your strength and salvation,
in his presence is your peace.
The peace of the Lord be always with you.
And also with you.

Blessing

The Almighty God give you strength to stand against all evil,
the Saviour deliver you from harm,
the Spirit inspire and guide you:
and the blessing of God Almighty, the Father, the Son and the Holy Spirit, be upon you and remain with you always.
Amen.

14 SEPTEMBER

Holy Cross Day

After Constantine became the emperor, he made Christianity the religion of the Roman Empire: the major persecutions of Christians ceased and the pilgrims started going to Rome and to the Holy Land. Constantine's mother Helena made a pilgrimage to the Holy Land in 326 and stayed for almost three years; she funded the building of churches on the Mount of Olives and at Bethlehem. It is said she also discovered the cross of Christ. A basilica was built on the site of the Holy Sepulchre. The symbol of the cross became the main symbol of Christianity. We remember this day as a day of thanksgiving for the love and saving power of our God.

Readings

Numbers 21:4-9
Philippians 2:6-11
John 3:13-17

Opening prayer

God of our salvation, as we give thanks for the discovery by Helena of the holy cross, may we ever rejoice in your saving love revealed in your Son, our Saviour. May the cross inspire our lives and point us to the gift of life eternal: we ask this in the name of him who died for us, Jesus Christ, our Lord.

Intercessions

Ever loving God, we give thanks for St Helena and ask your blessing upon all churches and people dedicated in her name and on churches dedicated in the name of the Holy Cross.
We ask your blessing upon the churches in the Holy Land, remembering especially the Holy Sepulchre, and we pray for all pilgrims.

We ask your blessing upon all who are suffering or facing persecution for their faith.
May we know your steadfast love as revealed through the sacrifice of Christ for us.
In the name of Jesus,
you are our strength and our salvation.

Ever loving God, we pray for the people of the island of St Helena.
We remember places with her name and pray for St Helen Auckland, St Helens in Merseyside, St Helens on the Isle of Wight, and St Helen's in East Sussex: we remember all individuals who share her name.
We pray that all who wear the cross may use it as a symbol of your love and not just a piece of jewellery.
We pray for all who need to know your power to save and your healing grace.
In the name of Jesus,
you are our strength and our salvation.

Ever loving God, we ask your blessing upon the communities to which we belong, and on for all who help us to experience belonging to a common union.
We give thanks for all who welcome newcomers and make them feel wanted and respected.
We pray for our homes, friends and loved ones, that in our love for each other we may know more of your love for us .
We pray for those who find it difficult to make friends or to be friendly.
In the name of Jesus,
you are our strength and our salvation.

Ever loving God, we remember all who are struggling with life, all who feel they cannot cope any longer and need help.
We pray for those who have been injured or hurt through acts of violence and for those betrayed in love.
We pray for those who feel scorned and rejected by those around them.
We ask your blessing upon friends and loved ones who are ill or in difficulties . . .
In the name of Jesus,
you are our strength and our salvation.

Ever loving God, we rejoice in your saving power through the cross
and give thanks for your gift of eternal life.
We remember before you friends and loved ones departed from us . . .
Merciful Father,
accept these prayers for the sake of your Son, our Saviour, Jesus Christ.
Amen.

The peace

Do not let your heart be troubled.
Believe in the love of the Creator,
and in Jesus Christ who has conquered death.
The peace of the Lord be always with you.
And also with you.

Blessing

May you find in Christ crucified
the power of God's love,
the forgiveness of sins,
the gift of eternal life:
and the blessing of God Almighty, the Father, the Son and the Holy Spirit, be upon you and remain with you always.
Amen.

15 SEPTEMBER

Cyprian

Cyprian was born about the year 200 in Carthage. He became an orator, teacher of rhetoric and an advocate in the courts before becoming a Christian about the year 245. He gave up all pagan writings and concentrated his studies on the Scriptures and Christian commentaries, especially those of Tertullian. Within a few years he became a priest, and in 248 was made Bishop of Carthage by the choice of the people. Almost immediately, he had to face the Decian persecutions. He fled to safety but guided his flock by correspondence. He sought for compassion and leniency towards returning apostates which was against the harder approach of the Pope. When the persecutions began again under Emperor Valerian, he refused the command for all to take part in pagan worship. As a result of this he was sent into exile, then condemned to death and beheaded in the year 258.

Readings

Jeremiah 11:18-20
1 Peter 4:12-end
Matthew 18:18-22

Opening prayer

God of grace, we give thanks for Cyprian's revealing of your love and care as he sought to protect his people being forced into pagan practices. Strengthen and guide your Church at this time to stand against the onslaught of cynicism and secularisation and to be firm in the faith: we ask this in the name of Christ, our Lord.

Intercessions

God our Shepherd, guide us and protect us against all that seeks to prevent us from loving and serving you.

May our priests and pastors have the sensitivity to know what pressures many of us work under.
We pray for those who are not allowed to express their faith, and are forbidden to pray for others.
With the rising tide of Islam, we pray that we may stand firm but be compassionate.
Lord, we trust in you,
hear us and help us.

God our Shepherd, we pray for world governments struggling with the rapid changes and the movement of people.
We ask your blessing upon all who are seeking to protect the environment and endangered species.
We remember those who stand up for indigenous people that are being oppressed.
We pray for all who are at risk for being outspoken or standing against tyrants and despots.
Lord, we trust in you,
hear us and help us.

God our Shepherd, we give thanks for your love revealed to us through our loved ones.
We pray for children who have just started school and those beginning a new term.
We pray for the young members of our community and for the pressures upon them.
We pray for homes where there are difficulties in relationships and for those who are leaving home for the first time.
Lord, we trust in you,
hear us and help us.

God our Shepherd, we remember all suffering from famine or flood.
We pray for nations in upheaval and for all who have become refugees and homeless people.
We remember all who do not have sufficient resources to survive, and pray for all relief agencies.
We remember before you friends and loved ones who are ill or in need . . .
Lord, we trust in you,
hear us and help us.

God our Shepherd, we remember that you have created us out of love and for your love.
We give you thanks for the sacrifice of Cyprian for others and pray for all the faithful departed.
We remember in your presence loved ones and friends departed, and pray for them in the stillness . . .
Merciful Father,
accept these prayers for the sake of your Son, our Saviour, Jesus Christ.
Amen.

The peace

God enfold you in his love,
be your strength in time of fear,
and deliver you from all evil.
The peace of the Lord be always with you.
And also with you.

Blessing

The life-giving God go with you,
the love of the Saviour encompass you,
the light of the Spirit guide you:
and the blessing of God Almighty, the Father, the Son and the Holy Spirit, be upon you and remain with you always.
Amen.

16 SEPTEMBER

Ninian

Ninian is the first saint we know of in what is today Scotland. He lived and worked nearly two centuries before Columba on Iona. The monastery he built was dedicated to St Martin of Tours: it was built in stone which was unusual for a Briton. But the remains of his monastery at Whithorn witness to the fact that Candida Casa was built for a community of monks. The name Candida Casa was because it had a white appearance so was called the White House, giving the name to Whithorn which means the same. It's interesting that St Hilda's foundation on the opposite coast was also a white house – that is, Whitby. It appears that Ninian worked around the Galloway area and up into the Stirling, Perth, Fife and Forfar areas. Though he was a bishop, there is no certainty that he went to Rome or to train under Martin of Tours, though both were possible and the early Christian monks were good travellers. He died about the year 432.

Readings

Jeremiah 4:1-10
Acts 13:46-49
Mark 16:15-end

Opening prayer

God, who called Ninian to proclaim the Good News to the Britons and Picts, grant that we may realise that the gospel needs to be proclaimed in our time and that hearts and minds need to know and live by your compassion and love for all: we ask this in the name of our Lord, Jesus Christ.

Intercessions

God of grace, we give thanks for Ninian and pray for all churches dedicated in his name; we pray for the Church in Whithorn and in Dumfries and Galloway.

We ask your blessing upon all evangelists and preachers.
We pray for those who are in training to be priests and ministers and ask your blessing upon those who teach them.
We pray for all who quietly witness to your love by their example and lives.
God of glory,
in your goodness, hear us.

God of grace, we give you thanks for the beauty and wonders of creation.
May we respect the uniqueness of each creature and the preciousness of life.
We pray for those who work to provide for our needs, that they may have a fair wage and not be used as cheap labour.
We remember all who have no work and are in need.
God of glory,
in your goodness, hear us.

God of grace, we give you thanks for the land in which we live and for all who have made a good land.
We pray for those who seek to build up our community and strengthen its bonds of fellowship and compassion.
We ask your blessing upon our homes, our workplaces, our loved ones and our friends.
We pray for any who feel left out of the community and lack friendship, that they may be made to feel welcome and wanted.
God of glory,
in your goodness, hear us.

God of grace, we pray for those who are in need in any way.
We remember those unable to cope alone and in need of care and attention.
We remember all who are ill, and we name before you, Lord, those known to us . . .
We ask your blessing upon all who express their compassion and love for the needy through their work or actions.
God of glory,
in your goodness, hear us.

God of grace, we give thanks for Ninian and the monastery at Whithorn and pray that all who served you faithfully there may rest in peace.
We pray for our friends and loved ones departed . . . that you will bring us all to a joyful resurrection and newness of life.
Merciful Father,
accept these prayers for the sake of your Son, our Saviour, Jesus Christ.
Amen.

The peace

God surround you with his peace,
give you peace in your heart,
in your minds and in your life.
The peace of the Lord be always with you.
And also with you.

Blessing

The presence of the Father Almighty encircle you,
the peace of Christ the Saviour enfold you,
the power of the Holy Spirit be upon you:
and the blessing of God Almighty, the Father, the Son and the Holy Spirit, be upon you and remain with you always.
Amen.

17 SEPTEMBER

Hildegard

Hildegard was born in 1098 at Bokelheim in Germany. She was educated from the age of eight by a recluse called Jutta, then at fifteen became a Benedictine nun. It was at the age of 32 she began to have revelations and visions. In 1136 she succeeded Jutta as Abbess of Diessenberg and was told to write down her visions. She called her visions *Savias*, meaning the one who knows the way of the Lord. During this time her community grew too large for its convent and they moved to Rupertsberg, near Bingen, from where she helped to reform other convents. She wrote poems, hymns and a morality play, as well as writing about her visions. She was interested in medicine and natural history and wrote on the elements, plants, trees, minerals, fishes, birds, quadrupeds and reptiles: an amazing achievement for its time, especially for a cloistered nun. She wrote commentaries on the Gospels, the lives of the saints and on the Rule of St Benedict. She was also a musician and an artist. Though she had repeated illnesses and physical weakness, she lived until 1179.

Readings

Song of Solomon 8:6, 7
1 Corinthians 2:3-9
Luke 10:21-24

Opening prayer

Generous God, as you granted to Hildegard a glimpse of your glory, we pray that our eyes may be open to your presence, our hearts to your love and our lips to proclaim your praise: we ask this in the love of Christ, our Lord.

Intercessions

God our Creator, as we give thanks for Hildegard, may we rejoice in the beauty and wonder of your creation and have love and awe for all you have made.
May the Church proclaim your love for the world and a respect for all its creatures.
We ask your blessing upon all visionaries who through their insights improve our world and lead us to a better awareness of you and of our purpose on earth.
We ask you to guide all who lead our worship, that they may give us a sense of wonder, awe and love for you.
Open our eyes to your presence,
and our hearts to your love.

God our Creator, all things come from you and we are responsible to you for the way we use your creation.
We ask your blessing upon all who call us to live in simplicity and unity, and pray we may heed their words.
We pray for the World Wildlife Fund and for those who work in the protection and preservation of creatures.
We remember those who work in nature conservation and those who monitor and care for our air, our rivers and our seas.
Open our eyes to your presence,
and our hearts to your love.

God our Creator, we thank you for our lives and pray we may use them in the service of others and to your glory.
We ask your blessing upon all who work for the building up of unity and fellowship in our area and in the worldwide community.
We ask your blessing upon our loved ones and homes, for our peace and enjoyment of each other.
We pray that we may see you in all whom we meet and be open to your coming to us.
Open our eyes to your presence,
and our hearts to your love.

God our Creator, we pray for all those who are struggling with poverty or illness.
We ask your blessing upon those who have the care of them, and are often suffering with them.

We remember those who are working in the healing professions, and pray for our doctors and nurses.
We pray to you for friends and loved ones who are suffering or in need . . .
Open our eyes to your presence,
and our hearts to your love.

God our Creator, we come from you, we belong to you, we return to you.
We give thanks for Hildegard, for her writings and wisdom and for all your saints in glory.
We remember friends and loved ones who are departed from us.
Merciful Father,
accept these prayers for the sake of your Son, our Saviour, Jesus Christ. Amen.

The peace

Rejoice in God's love for the world.
Rest in the love of the Saviour.
Know the power of the Holy Spirit.
And abide in God's peace.
The peace of the Lord be always with you.
And also with you.

Blessing

God the Creator give you joy in his creation,
Christ our Lord help you to love the world as he loves it,
God the Holy Spirit guide you into ways of peace:
and the blessing of God Almighty, the Father, the Son and the Holy Spirit, be upon you and remain with you always.
Amen.

20 SEPTEMBER

John Coleridge Patteson

John Coleridge Patteson was born in London in 1827. He was educated at Eton, where he came under the influence of George Augustus Selwyn. He was ordained and when he was 28 left Britain to begin his work among the islands of the South Pacific, becoming the first Bishop of Melanesia. He sought to empower the indigenous people to act as evangelists. His aim was that these would be then ordained and share the gospel within their communities and culture. This was fruitful and the faith spread rapidly. At this time the Melanesians were troubled by European slave-traders. When Bishop Coleridge landed on the island of Nukapu to show that not all white people were slave traders, he and his fellow workers were attacked. Bishop Coleridge and two of his helpers were killed. But his murder proved to be the seed of the Melanesian Church which grew from strength to strength.

Readings

2 Chronicles 24:17-21
Acts 7:55-end
Matthew 16:24-26

Opening prayer

God, who created all people in your love, we thank you for the call and obedience of John Coleridge Patteson and his work in Melanesia with the Good News of the gospel. May we be aware of your call and do your will in our daily lives: we ask this in the name of Christ, our Lord.

Intercessions

God, you have created us for a purpose: may we each seek to fulfil
our calling in the service of the world and humankind.

We remember all who have given their lives in the service of others, and pray for any that are at risk in fulfilling their calling.
We pray for our parish and its outreach to all within it, and ask your blessing upon those who seek to teach the young or any enquirers.
We pray for the work of the Church in Melanesia and for the Melanesian Brotherhood.
Lord, you have called us,
make us worthy of our calling.

God, we ask your blessing upon all who seek to maintain law and order, for the police and the work of the social services.
We remember those who work to bring peace to peoples and nations and we pray for the United Nations.
We ask your blessing upon the work of the Red Cross and on all who help in areas of emergency, in time of disaster.
We pray for those who are working among the street children and orphans of our world.
Lord, you have called us,
make us worthy of our calling.

God, you called us to learn of your love through our families and friends; we ask your blessing upon our homes and on all who are dear to us.
We pray for families and relationships that are breaking down, where there is a lack of trust or love.
We remember especially the elderly and the young who feel rejected or unwanted.
We ask your blessing upon the Children's Society and the social services.
Lord, you have called us,
make us worthy of our calling.

God, we remember all who feel thwarted in life through injury, disability or illness, and especially those who are embittered.
We remember those who are not at peace with themselves or with others, and who make life difficult for those around them.
We ask your blessing upon all who are ill and the families that are suffering through loss of income and sorrow for the loved one.
We ask your blessing upon all known to us who are ill or troubled in

any way and we name them before you . . .
Lord, you have called us,
make us worthy of our calling.

God, we give thanks for the witness of John Coleridge Patteson and for his belief in life eternal.
We pray for him and all our loved ones departed . . .
Merciful Father,
accept these prayers for the sake of your Son, our Saviour, Jesus Christ. Amen.

The peace

All who love God should love his creation.
All who seek peace should share his peace with others.
The peace of the Lord be always with you.
And also with you.

Blessing

Put your trust in God; in him alone is your hope,
in him alone is true peace,
in him alone is the fullness of joy;
put your trust in God:
and the blessing of God Almighty, the Father, the Son and the Holy Spirit, be upon you and remain with you always.
Amen.

25 SEPTEMBER

Lancelot Andrewes

Lancelot Andrewes was born in 1555 at Barking. He studied at the Merchant Taylors' School and Pembroke Hall in Cambridge. In 1580 he was elected a fellow of Pembroke. After he was ordained priest in 1581, he served in various parishes until he was appointed Bishop of Chichester in 1605, then Bishop of Ely, and finally the Bishop of Winchester in 1619. He was present at the Hampton Court Conference in 1604, which sought reforms within the Church of England. He translated much of the Old Testament for what became the King James Version of the Bible. His preaching, prayers and writing all reflected his holy life and his gentle nature. He had prepared a notebook of *Private Prayers* for his own use in prayer and meditation which was published after his death and was of great use within the Church.

Readings

Isaiah 1:6-18
1 Peter 5:1-4
Matthew 10:16-22

Opening prayer

Lord, encouraged by the prayers of Lancelot Andrewes, may we abide in you: take our minds and think through them,
take our hands and bless through them,
take our mouths and speak through them,
take our hearts and love through them:
we ask this in the name of Christ, our Saviour.

Intercessions

Lord God, perfect in your Church all that is lacking in its gifts:
of faith increase it,
of hope strengthen it,
and of love rekindle it.

As we give thanks for Lancelot Andrewes, we pray for the dioceses of Winchester, Chichester and Ely, for their bishops and for all who reside in the area.
We ask your blessing upon all who teach people to pray and to meditate.
Hear us, O Lord,
guide us and help us.

Lord God, may we act with integrity and responsibility for the wellbeing of all creation.
May we not misuse or waste the earth's resources or pollute the environment in any way.
We pray for those who work to provide sufficient food and water to impoverished areas.
We remember those who strive to bring medical care and make good housing available to all.
Hear us, O Lord,
guide us and help us.

Lord God, let this day add some good deed or knowledge to each of us.
We ask your blessing upon our local colleges, schools and nurseries.
We pray for our local tradespeople and suppliers of our needs.
We ask your blessing upon our homes, our families and friends.
Hear us, O Lord,
guide us and help us.

Lord God, we give thanks and pray for all who care for the ill and infirm, and ask your blessing upon our hospitals and their staff.
We pray for those who are finding life difficult and are unable to cope alone.
We bring before you, Lord, friends and loved ones who are ill or in need . . .
We pray that we may all know your power, your peace and your abiding presence.
Hear us, O Lord,
guide us and help us.

Lord God, blessed are you, for you turn the shadow of night to the morning of a new day, and renew your creation.
We pray for all our loved ones departed, that they may walk in newness of life in your kingdom . . .
Merciful Father,
accept these prayers for the sake of your Son, our Saviour, Jesus Christ.
Amen.

The peace

Abide in God's love and know he is with you,
abide in God and rest in his peace.
The peace of the Lord be always with you.
And also with you.

Blessing

God give you grace to be what he created you to be,
God empower you to do what he would have you do:
and the blessing of God Almighty, the Father, the Son and the Holy Spirit, be upon you and remain with you always.
Amen.

27 SEPTEMBER

Vincent de Paul

Vincent de Paul was born in 1581 at Ranquine in Gascony, France. He was educated by the Franciscans and ordained priest at the early age of 20. In 1609 he was falsely charged with stealing: as a result of this, he resolved to devote the rest of his life and all he owned to the service of the poor. He founded the Congregation of Priests of the Mission (Lazarists). With the help of Louise de Marillac, they founded the Sisters of Charity, the first community for women that was not enclosed, and who worked for the relief of the poor. Vincent worked for the relief of galley slaves, convicts and the victims of war and many other deprived people. He died in 1660.

Readings

Isaiah 58:6-11
1 Corinthians 1:25-end
Matthew 25:34-40

Opening prayer

God of love and compassion, who called Vincent de Paul to express your love for all, may our hearts also be warm and compassionate, that by word and deed we may be of help to those in need: we ask this in the name of Christ, our Lord.

Intercessions

Loving Lord, we pray for the Lazarists, the Daughters of Charity, and the Society of Vincent de Paul and their care for the needy.
We pray for the Church working among oppressed, deprived and suffering people.
May your Church reveal your love and compassion for all and be a healing element in the world.

We pray for our local church and its share in this work and its proclaiming of the gospel.
Compassionate God,
hear our prayer.

Loving Lord, we ask your blessing upon all who work to bring freedom and justice for all people and pray for Amnesty International.
We remember all who work with refugees, and those who live in refugee camps and pray for the Red Cross, Christian Aid, CAFOD and all relief agencies.
We pray for all who enrich our world by their talents: musicians, artists, poets, architects, and gardeners.
May we do what we can to make the world a better place this week.
Compassionate God,
hear our prayer.

Loving Lord, we give thanks for all who have shared their lives and love with us and have enriched us by their goodness, and we ask your blessing upon them.
We pray for those who are good neighbours and care for those around them in their needs.
We ask your blessing upon all who give of their time and talents to build up community life.
We pray for any who feel they are outsiders, and that we may help to make them welcome.
Compassionate God,
hear our prayer.

Loving Lord, we remember all who have suffered through the greed of large industries.
We pray for those who live under corrupt regimes, those who are used as slave labour and those imprisoned on false charges.
We pray for all suffering and captive peoples.
We ask your blessing upon all those who are ill, and we remember before you friends and loved ones in their suffering . . .
Compassionate God,
hear our prayer.

Loving Lord, we rejoice that, in you, life is eternal, sorrow turns to joy and darkness gives way to light.
We give thanks for Vincent de Paul and all your saints in glory.
We remember friends and loved ones who are departed from us . . .
Merciful Father,
accept these prayers for the sake of your Son, our Saviour, Jesus Christ.
Amen.

The peace

God is full of compassion and mercy,
his love never ends:
he seeks to hold you and keep you in his peace.
The peace of the Lord be always with you.
And also with you.

Blessing

In God's presence is the fullness of joy,
he surrounds you with his love,
and upholds you in life:
and the blessing of God Almighty, the Father, the Son and the Holy Spirit, be upon you and remain with you always.
Amen.

OCTOBER

4 OCTOBER

Francis of Assisi

Francis was born in 1181, the son of a wealthy cloth merchant from Assisi and a French mother. He was baptised John, but given the name Francesco by his father, and this is the name he became known by. Francis as a young man fought in the war between Assisi and Perugia. Francis was taken prisoner for a year. He came home seriously ill. It was while at the ruined church of St Damiano, and looking at the Byzantine-style crucifix, that he heard a voice saying, 'Go and repair my house which is fallen down.' Francis sold some of his father's cloths to help to fund the repairs of St Damiano. This caused a great argument between him and his father. Francis renounced his inheritance, even the clothes he stood up in and began to embrace a life of poverty. For a while he lived alone, but was then joined by seven companions. They had no possessions, except for a few books, and lived in extreme poverty. Their primitive Rule was accepted by Rome in 1210. They spent their lives caring for the poor and preaching the gospel. Francis suddenly found himself the leader of a greater number of Friars. He helped Clare to found the community of the 'Poor Clares'. His love for Christ and for nature showed in all that he did. In 1224 he wrote the Canticle of the Sun. In the same year, while praying at La Verna, he received the stigmata, that are the wounds of the crucified Christ on his body. He died in 1226.

Readings

Song of Solomon 8:6, 7
Galatians 6:14-end
Luke 12:22-34

Opening prayer

Most High and Glorious God, as we give thanks for St Francis,
enlightten our lives,
grant us a sure faith,

a certain hope, and perfect love,
that in all we do we may fulfil your will: in the love of Jesus Christ, our Lord.

Intercessions

Lord, make us instruments of your peace: may we bring the light of the gospel to darkened lives and the darkness of the world.
We pray for all who have lost faith in themselves, in other people and in you, O God.
We remember all who have lost hope and live in the darkness of sorrow and fear.
We ask your blessing upon all who seek to bring light and love to the world.
We pray for all who are Franciscans, for churches dedicated in the name of St Francis, for the church in Assisi and all pilgrims there.
Lord, in the darkness,
may your light shine.

Lord, make us instruments of your peace.
Bless all who work for peace, share peace and live in peace.
We ask your blessing upon Elizabeth our Queen, our government, and the leaders of nations.
We pray for the work of the United Nations and for peace-keeping forces throughout the world.
We pray for all who seek to heal divisions and breakdowns in relationships or trust.
Lord, in the darkness,
may your light shine.

Lord, make us instruments of your peace, in our homes, in our communities.
May we work for the wellbeing and respect for all around us.
We pray for people and homes where there is unrest, tension and lack of trust.
We ask your blessing upon our families and friends, that they may live in loving fellowship and peace.
Lord, in the darkness,
may your light shine.

Lord, make us instruments of your peace.
Where there is injury, may we bring the healing of forgiveness.
Where there is doubt, may we help to encourage faith.
Where there is despair, may we help to bring hope.
Where there is sadness, may we bring your joy.
We pray for friends and loved ones who are ill . . .
Lord, in the darkness,
may your light shine.

Lord, in the darkness, may your light shine and open to us the promise of your abiding love and that in dying we are born to eternal life.
We pray for Francis, for all the faithful departed, and we remember our loved ones who are in your peace . . .
Merciful Father,
accept these prayers for the sake of your Son, our Saviour, Jesus Christ.
Amen.

The peace

God is your protector,
your guardian and defender,
your safe haven and your peace.
The peace of the Lord be always with you.
And also with you.

Blessing

Praise God, stand in awe of him,
honour him in all that you do,
glorify him forever:
and the blessing of God Almighty, the Father, the Son and the Holy Spirit, be upon you and remain with you always.
Amen.

6 OCTOBER

William Tyndale

William Tyndale was born in Gloucestershire about the year 1494. He studied at Magdalen Hall, Oxford from 1510 until 1515 and then at Cambridge. He was gifted at languages and started to translate the Scriptures into contemporary English: however, he was thwarted in this by the Bishop of London. He left England in 1524, never to return: he settled in Hamburg and continued his work on the Scriptures. He had the New Testament printed in Cologne and shipped to England in 1526. His translation was seen as subversive by the clergy and, at the instigation of Thomas More, it was banned and burnt. He spent much time after this revising his text and writing theological works. This work of his would prove to be a basic working text for those who produced the King James Bible. During this time various agents were seeking to have him condemned for heresy. Finally, he was imprisoned in Brussels. He was strangled to death and then burnt at the stake in 1536. His last words were: 'Lord, open the King of England's eyes.'

Readings

Proverbs 8:4-11
2 Timothy 3:12-end
John 15:18-21

Opening prayer

God our Creator, we give you thanks for William Tyndale and his translation of the Scriptures: may your word be a lantern to our feet and a light to our path. In reading and meditating on the Scriptures, may we be shown the way to faithfully serve you and rejoice in your unfailing love: we ask this in the name of Jesus Christ, our Lord.

Intercessions

God our Creator, we rejoice in the work of William Tyndale, and pray for those who shared their love of the Scriptures with us.
We pray for those who seek to make the Scriptures available in the language of the people, and we ask your blessing upon the Bible Society and Scripture Union.
We ask your blessing upon all who produce Bible commentaries and who teach the faith.
We pray for all preachers of the Word and teachers of Religious Education.
May your word be a lantern to our feet,
and a light to our path.

God our Creator, we ask your blessing upon those involved in communication.
We pray for a right use of the media in the way it produces information and influences our actions.
We pray for those who work in broadcasting or in the production of daily papers and news.
We ask your blessing upon those who seek to protect the freedom of speech.
May your word be a lantern to our feet,
and a light to our path.

God our Creator, we thank you for those who have shared their lives, their love and their talents with us, and we ask your blessing upon them.
We pray that we may be generous in the way we help others and have the humility to know when we need to accept help.
We pray for our homes, that they may reflect your love and peace.
We ask your blessing upon families that are struggling with their relationships or with poverty.
May your word be a lantern to our feet,
and a light to our path.

God our Creator, we remember all who are imprisoned through false charges or despotic rule.
We pray for those whose talents are thwarted by the environment they live in or by human prejudice.
We remember all who are suffering from poverty, violence or war.
We pray for those who are ill and remember before you, O Lord, friends and loved ones in their troubles . . .
May your word be a lantern to our feet,
and a light to our path.

God our Creator, you have created us out of your love and for your love.
We pray for all who have left this earth and returned to you and your love.
We remember William Tyndale, and we pray for friends and loved ones departed . . .
Merciful Father,
accept these prayers for the sake of your Son, our Saviour, Jesus Christ. Amen.

The peace

The Word of God dwell in your hearts,
set your hearts on fire with love for him,
and keep you in his peace.
The peace of the Lord be always with you.
And also with you.

Blessing

Live in praise of the Creator,
in the love of the Word of Life,
in the power of the Holy Spirit:
and the blessing of God Almighty, the Father, the Son and the Holy Spirit, be upon you and remain with you always.
Amen.

10 OCTOBER

Paulinus

Paulinus was one of a second group of monks sent by Pope Gregory to England in 601. When Edwin of Northumbria sought to marry Ethelburga, the Christian sister of the king of Kent, Paulinus was consecrated bishop and went to Northumbria with them as her chaplain and with the hope of converting Edwin to the faith. After some years, Paulinus baptised Edwin, his infant daughter and Hilda amongst others on Easter Day 627/28 in a wooden church erected for the purpose in York; this is where York Minster is built today. Many nobles and others now sought baptism. In the river Swale near Catterick and the river Glen at Yeavering in Northumbria were the sites of mass baptisms. Paulinus' mission was cut short by the death of Edwin at the battle of Hatfield Chase in 633. Paulinus returned to Kent with Queen Ethelburga. Here he acted as Bishop of Rochester for the rest of his life; he died in 644.

Readings

Isaiah 61:1-3a
Romans 15:17-21
Matthew 28:16-end

Opening prayer

God, who called Paulinus to come to this land, to preach, baptise and build up your Church, grant that by his example we may be encouraged to make known your love and help to reveal your glory in our lives: we ask this in the name of Christ, our Lord.

Intercessions

Loving Lord, as we give thanks for Paulinus and his proclamation of the gospel, we pray for the dioceses of York and of Rochester, and for all the people who live and work within them.

We ask your blessing upon those who are involved in the mission of the Church, and pray we may have a part in this work.
We pray for all who build up the Church through preaching, teaching and writing.
May we always be open to your presence and your love.
Holy Lord,
hear us and help us.

Loving Lord, we remember before you the world's poor, those deprived of food, clean water, education or basic human rights.
We pray for those who suffer through the greed of others and are used as cheap labour or work slaves.
We remember all who have left homes and land with the hope of a place where they will have freedom and not starve.
We pray for the work of the United Nations and world governments in their protection of human rights for all people.
Holy Lord,
hear us and help us.

Loving Lord, we give thanks for our homes and all who provide for their safety and needs.
We ask your blessing upon our loved ones, neighbours, and friends.
We pray for our schools and all places of learning and ask your blessing upon those who teach.
We pray that our environment will be protected for future generations.
Holy Lord,
hear us and help us.

Loving Lord, we pray for those who work in the caring professions.
We remember those seeking to bring peace to war-torn areas.
We pray for any who are not at peace or who are ill at this time.
We remember before you, Lord, those known to us who are ill or struggling in any way . . .
Holy Lord,
hear us and help us.

Loving Lord, we give you thanks for the gift of eternal life.
We pray for Paulinus and remember any who have died this week . . .

We pray that our loved ones departed may rejoice in your loving presence, and we remember them before you . . .
Merciful Father,
accept these prayers for the sake of your Son, our Saviour, Jesus Christ.
Amen.

The peace

The Lord is your strength and salvation,
the Lord is your hope and your joy,
the Lord is your life and your peace.
The peace of the Lord be always with you.
And also with you.

Blessing

The joy of God's creation be yours,
the joy of Christ's salvation be yours,
the joy of the indwelling Spirit be yours:
and the blessing of God Almighty, the Father, the Son and the Holy Spirit, be upon you and remain with you always.
Amen.

12 OCTOBER

Wilfrid of Ripon

Wilfrid was born in Northumbria of a noble family about the year 633. He was educated at Lindisfarne, proving to be a good scholar. He went on to Canterbury and then to Rome in 653. When he returned to England, he was made Abbot of Ripon at the invitation of the sub-king Alcfrith. Here he introduced the Rule of St Benedict, and the Roman method of calculating Easter. At the Synod of Whitby in 664 he was the main spokesman for the case of the Roman calculation of Easter, against the system from Lindisfarne and Iona. The Roman cause was successful and Alcfrith chose Wilfrid to be the Bishop of York. Due to a lack of Roman bishops, Wilfrid went to France to be consecrated by 12 Frankish bishops. But he stayed there too long and found when he returned in 666 that Chad had been appointed bishop in his place. He retired to Ripon but in 669 he was reinstated as Bishop of York by Archbishop Theodore. He had many fine churches built, notably at Hexham which was said to be the finest building north of the Alps, and a great church at Ripon. However, he fell foul of King Egfrith who had him imprisoned and later released on the condition that he left Northumbria. He did five years of missionary work in Sussex, the Isle of Wight, and Friesland. When he died in 709, he was buried in Ripon.

Readings

Malachi 2:5-7
1 Corinthians 1:18-25
Luke 5:1-11

Opening prayer

Holy Lord, we give you thanks and praise for Wilfrid, and the building up of the Church in this land. May we also take part in the building of your Church and proclaim your love for all of creation: we ask this in the name of Christ, our Lord.

Intercessions

Loving Lord, as we give thanks for Wilfrid, may we know you as our light and salvation and share in your saving work.
We ask your blessing upon the dioceses of York, of West Yorkshire and the Dales, and on the churches of Ripon Cathedral and Hexham Abbey, and we pray for all who live within these areas.
We remember all who are persecuted for their faith, all who are mocked or scorned, and pray for those tempted to lose heart.
We pray for unity within the Church among the diversity of peoples.
Holy and Mighty God,
we hope in you, we trust in you.

Loving Lord, we pray for Elizabeth our Queen, for Parliament and all in positions of power.
May those in power use their skills to bring peace and wellbeing to those who are in their charge.
We ask your blessing upon all who work to conserve and protect the resources of the earth and act with concern for future generations.
May we not waste or squander but live simply and enjoy the earth and its beauty.
Holy and Mighty God,
we hope in you, we trust in you.

Loving Lord, we ask your blessing upon our community and our homes, that we may live in peace and fellowship with one another.
We pray for our friends and our families, for their love and support for one another.
We pray for areas where loved ones are separated from each other through war, terrorism or disasters, and remember children left alone or as orphans.
We pray for those who work for everyone to have a decent education, home and water supply.
Holy and Mighty God,
we hope in you, we trust in you.

Loving Lord, we give thanks for your abiding presence in our lives and pray for all whose lives are darkened by doubt, guilt or fear.
We pray for all who are chronically ill or disabled in any way and for those who cannot cope on their own.

We pray for all the people who feel lost or unwanted within society and remember all who live on the streets and sleep rough.
We ask your blessing upon friends and loved ones who are ill . . .
Holy and Mighty God,
we hope in you, we trust in you.

Loving Lord, we rejoice in the power of the resurrection, praying for Wilfrid and all the saints in glory.
As we pray for the faithful departed, we remember before you our friends and loved ones in your heavenly kingdom.
Merciful Father,
accept these prayers for the sake of your Son, our Saviour, Jesus Christ. Amen.

The peace

In God is rest for the weary,
strength for the faint-hearted,
and peace for the troubled.
The peace of the Lord be always with you.
And also with you.

Blessing

God, who called you, make you worthy of your calling,
guide and strengthen you,
enfold you in his peace:
and the blessing of God Almighty, the Father, the Son and the Holy Spirit, be upon you and remain with you always.
Amen.

13 OCTOBER

Edward the Confessor

Edward was born about 1003, the son of Ethelred 'the Unready' and Emma, the sister of Richard the Duke of Normandy. Edward was educated at Ely and then in Normandy. He spent almost 30 years in Normandy as a political exile. He returned to England in 1041 and succeeded to the throne the following year. Edward was greatly concerned for peace and justice in his kingdom. He was a man of prayer and was generous towards the poor. His religious devotion led him to endow St Peter's Abbey on Thorney Island by the river Thames: now known as Westminster Abbey where most of his successors to the throne are buried. He died in 1066.

Readings

2 Samuel 23:1-8
2 Timothy 4:1-6
Luke 22:24-30

Opening prayer

Lord God, who called Edward to serve you as a king upon earth and witness to you by his life of prayer and love of the poor, may we strive for your kingdom to come in us and show our compassion upon all in need: we ask this in the love of Jesus Christ, our Lord.

Intercessions

King of Glory, we give you thanks for Edward the Confessor, for Westminster Abbey and for all who visit and worship there.
We ask your blessing upon those who share their faith through word and deed.
We remember all who quietly dedicate themselves to you in their daily lives.
We pray for all who are searching to know you and your peace in their lives: and pray that the Church may be of help to them.
Lord, your kingdom come,
on earth as it is in heaven.

King of Glory, we ask your blessing upon all rulers and those in positions of authority, and ask you to give them sensitivity and compassion.
We pray for Elizabeth our Queen, for our local and national government.
We pray for the city and people of London and for those who visit there.
We remember the poor, the homeless and refugees in our towns and cities.
Lord, your kingdom come,
on earth as it is in heaven.

King of Glory, we ask your blessing upon our lives, our homes and our loved ones.
We give thanks for those who supply our daily needs and who work to provide us with food and safety.
We pray for the work of the police, and the emergency services.
We ask your blessing upon all who are struggling within our community; where we can, may we be of some help.
Lord, your kingdom come,
on earth as it is in heaven.

King of Glory, we give thanks for all who witness to your love even when in pain or distress.
We pray for those who suffer through the cruelty or mindlessness of others.
We remember those who have lost faith through war or some event in their lives.
We ask your blessing upon all who are ill or suffering at this time, and we name before you those we know and love . . .
Lord, your kingdom come,
on earth as it is in heaven.

King of Glory, we rejoice that we are one in you with the saints in glory.
We give thanks for the faith and witness of Edward the Confessor, and all the blessing that Westminster Abbey has been a help in.
We pray for the faithful departed and remember especially before you those who are dear to us . . .

Merciful Father,
accept these prayers for the sake of your Son, our Saviour, Jesus Christ.
Amen.

The peace

God's presence is with us,
his light shines in the darkness of our world,
he seeks to guide us into the ways of peace.
The peace of the Lord be always with you.
And also with you.

Blessing

Sing to God and make music in your heart to the Lord,
he is our creator and our salvation;
rejoice, for God is the Lord who rescues us from death:
and the blessing of God Almighty, the Father, the Son and the Holy Spirit, be upon you and remain with you always.
Amen.

15 OCTOBER

Teresa of Avila

Teresa was born of a noble Spanish family in Avila in 1515. She was educated at home until the death of her mother and then by Augustinian nuns. At the age of 21 she became a Carmelite nun in the Convent of the Incarnation at Avila. Her writings tell of her struggles and difficulties in her prayer life; she constantly believed she had failed God. After 25 years under the unreformed Rule, she began to reform the Order with the help of St Peter of Alcantara and St John of the Cross. She sought to establish Houses based on poverty, solitude and manual work; she founded 17 such Houses in her lifetime. Her writings on mystical and ascetical theology led her to be declared a Doctor of the Church in 1970. In Spain, they say that to understand St Teresa you have to look at Castile and its rough landscape and extremes between heat and cold. Teresa showed herself as an ordinary human being, loving and longing to be loved, and always aware of her failures. She died in 1582.

Readings

Wisdom 7:7-15
Romans 8:22-27
John 15:1-8

Opening prayer

God, who called Teresa of Avila to a life of prayer amidst hardship and poverty, help us to know the way to your presence is always open to us, wherever we are and whatever is happening to us: we ask this in the love of our Lord, Jesus Christ.

Intercessions

Loving Lord, you have created each of us for a purpose; help us to know what you would have us do.
When we fail you, Lord God, may we know you never fail us but love us with an everlasting love.
We ask your blessing upon all who struggle with prayer, and that they may have the courage and faith to continue.
We pray for all Carmelites and ask your blessing upon the Church in Spain.
Show us your love, O Lord,
and grant us your salvation.

Loving Lord, we pray for those who are overburdened with labour, the world's poor, and those used as cheap labour.
We pray for children sent out to beg or to steal and for all the street children of our world.
We ask your blessing upon all who work for the freedom and fair dealing of all; we pray for Fair Trade and all relief agencies.
May we who have received plenty not waste or squander what we have, and help others where we can.
Show us your love, O Lord,
and grant us your salvation.

Loving Lord, may our homes reflect your love and our common union with you.
We ask your blessing upon our loved ones, remembering especially any who are restless or not at peace with themselves.
We pray for our communities and that divisions and old wounds may be healed.
We ask your blessing upon all who are lonely and feel unloved or unwanted.
Show us your love, O Lord,
and grant us your salvation.

Loving Lord, we give thanks that you never leave us or forsake us, that you are with us in the darkness as well as the light and your love is an everlasting love.

We remember all who are plunged into uncertainty through illness or change in circumstances, all who feel lost or distressed.
We pray for all who are ill, and name before you those whom we know . . .
We ask your blessing upon all who assist in healing and who bring peace and love to those in need.
Show us your love, O Lord,
and grant us your salvation.

Loving Lord, we give you praise for the life and writings of Teresa of Avila and for all your saints in glory.
We ask your blessing upon our loved ones departed, as we remember them before you . . .
Merciful Father,
accept these prayers for the sake of your Son, our Saviour, Jesus Christ. Amen.

The peace

Lord, you made us for yourself;
may we find our rest and peace in you.
The peace of the Lord be always with you.
And also with you.

Blessing

God, in his grace and goodness,
give you his peace in your hearts and minds,
in your homes and in all that you do:
and the blessing of God Almighty, the Father, the Son and the Holy Spirit, be upon you and remain with you always.
Amen.

17 OCTOBER

Ignatius of Antioch

Ignatius was probably born in Syria about the year 35. He became the Bishop of Antioch, the third largest city in the Roman Empire, about the year 69. Little is known about him until after his arrest during the persecution of Christians by Trajan. His final journey to Rome was under military guard. At Smyrna he met Polycarp and wrote some of his epistles. His epistles reveal a passionate commitment to Christ, and the importance of keeping unity within the Church. In the epistles he called himself a disciple and a 'bearer of God' through his ordination as bishop and the celebrating of the Eucharist. He wrote again at Troas, and the last of his seven epistles was written to the Church in Rome as he prepared for being put to death. He was thrown to the wild beasts, possibly in the Colosseum about the year 107.

Readings

Isaiah 43:1-7
Philippians 3:7-12
John 6:52-58

Opening prayer

Gracious God, we give thanks for the life, witness and martyrdom of Ignatius of Antioch, and pray that we may stand firm in the faith which we have received and encourage others to do likewise. In the face of indifference or persecution, may we find our strength in you: we ask this in the name of our Saviour, Jesus Christ.

Intercessions

Lord God, you are our strength and salvation: as we give you thanks and praise for Ignatius of Antioch, we pray for the Church wherever it is subject to persecution and oppression.
We remember Christians who are exiled or imprisoned for their beliefs and those whose lives or wellbeing are endangered.

We ask your blessing upon all who teach the faith in word, in writings or by their example.
We pray for those who work for the unity of the Church and the unity of humankind.
Lord, our Saviour,
hear us and help us.

Lord God, we give thanks for our land and its freedom, and pray for all who protect it and keep it in peace.
We pray for the oppressed and poor people of our world, that they may be respected and given new hope and freedom.
We remember all who suffer from injustice or tyranny and whose lives are greatly restricted.
We ask your blessing upon the United Nations and all peace-keeping forces.
Lord, our Saviour,
hear us and help us.

Lord God, we give thanks for all who have loved us and cared for us, and pray for our families and our friends.
We pray for all young people and remember especially any who are not in a loving and caring environment.
We pray for people who are in poor housing, or in danger of losing their homes.
We remember all who give their time and talents in building up community life and improving the world around them.
Lord, our Saviour,
hear us and help us.

Lord God, we give thanks for all who work in the healing professions and ask your blessing upon our local doctors and nurses.
We pray for those who work in the rescue services and those who deal with disasters.
We ask your blessing upon all who are distressed, depressed or despairing.
We pray for all who are ill and remember before you, O Lord God, those who are known to us.
Lord, our Saviour,
hear us and help us.

Lord God, we give thanks that you are our strength and our salvation: that all who come to you shall not perish but have eternal life.
We rejoice in the fellowship of St Ignatius of Antioch and all your saints.
We ask your blessing upon our loved ones departed . . .
may we share with them in your eternal glory.
Merciful Father,
accept these prayers for the sake of your Son, our Saviour, Jesus Christ.
Amen.

The peace

In God is our peace.
In him is the hope of all creation.
The peace of the Lord be always with you.
And also with you.

Blessing

God give you courage and hope in your troubles,
and know that nothing shall separate you from the love of God in Christ Jesus our Lord:
and the blessing of God Almighty, the Father, the Son and the Holy Spirit, be upon you and remain with you always.
Amen.

19 OCTOBER

Henry Martyn

Henry Martyn was born in Truro in 1781. When he went to Cambridge he became a committed evangelical, with an interest in Christian mission. He was encouraged in this through his friendship with Charles Simeon. In 1805 he went as a chaplain to the East India Company. It was expected that his ministry would be to the expatriates in Calcutta. But he went about learning the local languages and customs and started to work among the indigenous peoples, preaching and teaching in mission schools. He supervised the translation of the New Testament into Hindustani, then Persian and Arabic. He left for Persia to continue the work in the spreading of the gospel through preaching, teaching and mission schools. He died of tuberculosis in Armenia in 1812.

Readings

Isaiah 55:6-11
Acts 2:4, 22-36
Mark 16:15-end

Opening prayer

O God, who gave to Henry Martyn the desire to translate the Scriptures and proclaim the Good News, may we discover where you want us to be and what you want us to do and so fulfil our lives in your service: we ask this in the name of Jesus Christ, our Saviour.

Intercessions

Father of all creation, we pray for the Church in India and in Iran,
that it may proclaim your love for all and be an instrument of peace.
We pray for all who are full of the love of God and want to tell others the Good News.

Bless all who translate the Scriptures, who produce Bibles in local languages and who preach the Word.
May we dedicate our lives to showing your peace and love in all that we do.
Lord of life and love,
hear us and help us.

Father of all creation, we pray for areas of India and Iran where there is poverty and lack of resources, due to conflict or climate.
We pray for all who deal with the care of the earth and monitor areas of pollution or destruction, and ask your guidance upon all involved in genetic engineering.
We pray for those who enrich our world through their talents, and pray for artists, musicians, craftspeople and gardeners.
May we be careful in our use of the world's resources, and care for what is happening around us.
Lord of life and love,
hear us and help us.

Father of all creation, we ask your blessing upon the communities to which we belong, upon our homes and our families.
We pray for local community centres, places of recreation and renewal and for the people who look after them.
We ask your blessing upon all who teach in schools and in night classes, and that their students may be enriched by their teaching.
We remember all who work hard to provide a safe environment for young people now and in the future.
Lord of life and love,
hear us and help us.

Father of all creation, we remember those who have lost their homes through natural disasters or through war, and those who are now refugees.
We pray for those who feel their talents and their lives are being wasted, and all who are frustrated by what is around them.
We remember all who are disabled or restricted in any way and those who find it difficult to cope on their own.

We pray for all who are ill, and in the silence we bring those known to us before you, O Lord . . .
Lord of life and love,
hear us and help us.

Father of all creation, in your love you give us life and life eternal.
We give you thanks for Henry Martyn who proclaimed this Good News.
We remember our friends and loved ones departed who are now in your eternal kingdom . . .
Merciful Father,
accept these prayers for the sake of your Son, our Saviour, Jesus Christ.
Amen.

The peace

Rejoice in the Lord,
in his presence and his peace:
know that he is with you,
and enfolds you in his love.
The peace of the Lord be always with you.
And also with you.

Blessing

Be strong in the Lord,
be of good courage, through the power of his presence:
and the blessing of God Almighty, the Father, the Son and the Holy Spirit, be upon you and remain with you always.
Amen.

26 OCTOBER

Alfred the Great

Alfred was born in the Royal Palace at Wantage in 849. At an early age, his father sent him to Rome accompanied by many nobles, to be anointed and confirmed by Pope Leo. He came to the throne when he was 22 and helped to establish peace in both Church and state. As a young man he learnt the daily services of Hours off by heart, along with certain psalms and prayers. These he collected in a book which he kept by him day and night. He was a daily communicant and sought to translate many works into the vernacular. He was deeply aware of the dearth of teachers and education as a result of the Danish invasions. He gave half of his income to the founding of religious houses, which were to be centres of education, caring for the poor and for the ill. He was known as a learned and merciful king who encouraged learning. He died in 899.

Readings

2 Samuel 23:1-5
1 Timothy 2:1-6
John 18:33-37

Opening prayer

Lord God, ruler of all, we give you thanks for the life and witness of King Alfred. As we remember his thirst for learning, his faithfulness in worship and his hospitality towards the poor, may we follow his example and seek to love and serve you all our days: we ask this in the love of Christ, our Saviour.

Intercessions

King of Glory, as we give thanks for the faithfulness of Alfred in worship, we ask your blessing upon all who lead worship and for church musicians.
We pray for those who preach and minister within our communities.

We ask your blessing upon all who teach the faith through art, music and writing.
We pray for the Royal School of Church Music and for their work with choirs.
Your kingdom come,
on earth as it is in heaven.

King of Glory, as we give thanks for King Alfred's rule, we pray for Elizabeth our Queen and all the royal family.
We ask your blessing upon all rulers and those who serve in the governing of our world and in the keeping of peace.
We pray for areas where there is unrest or turmoil and for those working to bring calm and harmony.
We ask your blessing upon all who work to bring relief and justice to the world's poor and oppressed.
Your kingdom come,
on earth as it is in heaven.

King of Glory, we remember the hospitality of King Alfred, and pray that our homes may be places of welcome and hospitality.
We ask your blessing upon our loved ones, our neighbours and friends.
We pray for those who have left home and those who have been bereaved, that they may not be without help or friends.
We ask your blessing upon the social services and the homes that are provided for the homeless.
Your kingdom come,
on earth as it is in heaven.

King of Glory, as we remember the compassion of King Alfred, we pray for those who work in the caring professions and pray they may have compassion in all they do.
We pray for those who work in the National Health Service, for surgeons, doctors, nurses and all hospital workers.
We pray for friends and loved ones of the ill, that they may have patience and care.
We ask your blessing upon all ill and suffering people: and we pray by name for those who are dear to us . . .
Your kingdom come,
on earth as it is in heaven.

King of Glory, we remember King Alfred and all your saints in glory and we rejoice that we share a common union with them in you.
We pray for all the faithful departed and we remember before you our own loved ones . . .
Merciful Father,
accept these prayers for the sake of your Son, our Saviour, Jesus Christ.
Amen.

The peace

The Lord is King, let heaven and earth rejoice,
let the multitude of the isles be glad,
for he comes in peace to renew his people.
The peace of the Lord be always with you.
And also with you.

Blessing

May grace and peace be yours in abundance,
in the knowledge and love of God and our Lord Jesus Christ:
and the blessing of God Almighty, the Father, the Son and the Holy Spirit, be upon you and remain with you always.
Amen.

29 OCTOBER

James Hannington

James Hannington was born in 1847 into a Congregationalist family. Before going up to Oxford he had become a member of the Church of England. Once he was ordained, he served five years as a curate before being sent by the Church Missionary Society to Zanzibar and then to Uganda. He was consecrated as Bishop of East Equatorial Africa in 1884. Soon, with other Europeans and indigenous Christians, he began to go inland to spread the gospel. Mwanga, the King of Buganda, despised Christians as they would not sanction his moral laxity. As they came into his kingdom, he seized the whole group, torturing them for several days before butchering them all to death in 1885.

Readings

2 Chronicles 24:17-21
Romans 8:35-end
Matthew 10:28-39

Opening prayer

Gracious God, as we remember today James Hannington who became the first Bishop of Equatorial Africa and was martyred while seeking to reveal your presence in Uganda, may we be inspired by his life and witness to reach out in faith and help others to discover the joy of your presence: we ask this in the name of our Saviour, Jesus Christ.

Intercessions

God of grace and glory, we give thanks for the work and witness of
James Hannington and ask your blessing upon the Church
Missionary Society.
We pray for the Church in Eastern Equatorial Africa, its leaders and
its people, as they seek to build up their country.

We pray for churches struggling to survive, due to persecution or indifference.
We remember those in Uganda who died for their faith and pray for Christians who stand against evil regimes and despots.
God of glory,
in your grace and goodness, hear us.

God of grace and glory, we pray for the peoples of Uganda and for all who have died of AIDS.
We pray for children left without parents and without any form of support and often no home.
We pray for those who are seeking to be of help and for the medical services.
We ask your blessing upon all who work for peace and unity within the world, and remember the work of the United Nations.
God of glory,
in your grace and goodness, hear us.

God of grace and glory, we ask your blessing upon our homes and our loved ones.
May we reflect your love by the way we respect and care for all of creation.
We ask your blessing upon the area in which we live and those who maintain its essential services.
We pray for those who are new to the area, and that we may help to make them welcome and feel at home.
God of glory,
in your grace and goodness, hear us.

God of grace and glory, we pray for those who struggle against darkness, despair or fear, that they may know your light and love.
We pray for all who are captive to vice, addiction or greed, that they may find freedom from their captivity.
We remember those who are ill at home or in hospital, and we pray for your blessing upon . . .
God of glory,
in your grace and goodness, hear us.

God of grace and glory, we give thanks for James Hannington, the martyrs of Uganda and all your saints in glory.
We commend our loved ones departed to your love now and for eternity, and we remember them before you.
Merciful Father,
accept these prayers for the sake of your Son, our Saviour, Jesus Christ.
Amen.

The peace

The Lord is your defence and shield,
his presence is with you in all your troubles:
he is your strength and your peace.
The peace of the Lord be always with you.
And also with you.

Blessing

God give you grace to stand firm in the faith,
that you may reveal his love and presence in your life:
and the blessing of God Almighty, the Father, the Son and the Holy Spirit, be upon you and remain with you always.
Amen.

NOVEMBER

3 NOVEMBER

Richard Hooker

Richard Hooker was born about the year 1544 at Heavitree, Exeter. He attended Exeter Grammar School until 1559. He was then educated at Corpus Christi College, Oxford. He was made a fellow of the College. In 1579 he was ordained priest. Then in 1585 he became the Master of the Temple in London. He became a champion in showing the Church of England as the 'middle way' between the Roman Catholics and the Puritans. Of his writings the best known is *Of the Laws of Ecclesiastical Polity*. He demonstrated in his writings that the Church of England was rooted in the Scriptures and in tradition. He ended the latter part of his ministry as a parish priest, in 1591 leaving the Temple to be the priest at Boscomb in Wiltshire. Then in 1593 he became the parish priest of Bishopbourne near Canterbury. He died in the rectory there in 1600.

Readings

Ecclesiasticus 44:10-15
Titus 2:1-8
John 16:12-15

Opening prayer

Heavenly Father, as we give thanks for Richard Hooker, may we also rejoice in the diversity of the Anglican Church and its balance of Scripture and tradition. May we never treat lightly what men and women have defended with their lives: we ask this in the name of our Saviour, Jesus Christ.

Intercessions

God of all creation, help us to know we are one in your love.
We pray that we may discover the riches of the Scriptures and the depth in various church traditions: that in our diversity we may rejoice in our unity.

May the whole Church help to reveal a united world and work for peace and justice for all peoples.
We ask your blessing upon all who teach and preach from the Scriptures, that they may reveal your love for all of creation.
God, maker of heaven and earth,
in your love, hear us.

God of all creation, we ask your blessing upon the governments of the world, that they may work for unity and peace and not be divisive.
We ask your blessing upon all who work to protect indigenous communities and areas where there is a threat to the wellbeing of your creation.
We pray for those who work in scientific research, that they may find ways of providing for the needs and healing of people and the earth.
We give thanks for and ask your blessing upon all who provide us with our food, water and power.
God, maker of heaven and earth,
in your love, hear us.

God of all creation, we pray that our homes and the community in which we live may rejoice in a common unity.
May our homes be places of love, peace and joy.
We remember families that are divided, where there is little trust, betrayals, and violence.
We pray for children who are suffering because of disunity in their home.
God, maker of heaven and earth,
in your love, hear us.

God of all creation, we pray for those who are not at peace with themselves, with others, or with you.
We pray for homes where a member of the family is disturbed or distressed in any way.
We ask your blessing upon all who seek to bring peace, unity and love to homes that are divided.
We ask your blessing upon all who are ill or suffering at this time and we remember before you friends and loved ones in their troubles . . .
God, maker of heaven and earth,
in your love, hear us.

God of all creation, we give you thanks for the gift of life and life eternal, for your abiding love with us and your saving power.
As we give thanks for Richard Hooker, we pray for all who are departed from us and remember especially . . .
Merciful Father,
accept these prayers for the sake of your Son, our Saviour, Jesus Christ.
Amen.

The peace

The peace of God fill your heart and mind.
God's peace be upon you and in all your actions,
that you may be an instrument of his peace.
The peace of the Lord be always with you.
And also with you.

Blessing

Know that in God we share a common union,
God is our Maker;
God loves all of his creation,
God keeps us in his presence:
and the blessing of God Almighty, the Father, the Son and the Holy Spirit, be upon you and remain with you always.
Amen.

7 NOVEMBER

Willibrord of York

Willibrord was born in 658 in the kingdom of Northumbria, probably in the part that is now Yorkshire. He was educated at the monastery in Ripon under Wilfrid. When Wilfrid was forced to leave in 678, Willibrord left to study in Ireland. In 690 he returned to England. Encouraged by Egbert, he led a mission to Frisia with 12 monks to help. This mission prospered under the protection of Pippin II and the support of Pope Sergius. He went to Rome in 695 to be consecrated Bishop of Frisia and to become the Archbishop of Utrecht. He set about extending the Church, organising new dioceses, building new churches and founding new monasteries. He was known for his vigorous preaching and ministry and appeared to be always joyful. He was later joined by Boniface at the instigation of Gregory II. Willibrord laid the foundation for a century of English mission and influence on continental Christianity. The largest monastery he caused to be built was at Echternach in Luxembourg where he died in 739.

Readings

Isaiah 62:7-10
1 Corinthians 4:1-5
Matthew 28:16-end

Opening prayer

Holy Lord, we give thanks for the mission and ministry of Willibrord who helped to build up and extend the Church in Europe. May we, as he did, reveal your constant love and saving power in our day: we ask this in the name of our Saviour, Jesus Christ.

Intercessions

God of all, as we give thanks for Willibrord, may we seek to show the joy of knowing you in our lives.
May our faith be strengthened through daily prayer and the reading of the Scriptures.
We ask your blessing upon the Church in Northern Germany and in Holland.
We pray for the cathedral and diocese and people of Utrecht; and for the Church at Echternach and the people of Luxembourg.
Almighty and powerful God,
be our strength and our help.

God of all, we pray for all who are forced to leave their studying through warring factions or through illness.
We pray for students who cannot afford the courses they are on and so have to stop their studies: we remember those who have lost parents and their support.
We ask your blessing upon the schools in our area, for those who teach and for all who study.
We pray for children in nurseries or play schools, and for all who work with children.
Almighty and powerful God,
be our strength and our help.

God of all, may we be at home with you in our homes.
We ask your blessing upon our loves, families and friends.
We ask your blessing upon all who feel they are unloved and upon those who have hardened their hearts: that each may learn of your compassion and people who care for them.
We pray for those who have been separated from loved ones by war, disaster or illness and who feel lonely or lost.
Almighty and powerful God,
be our strength and our help.

God of all, remember those who go out to help in areas of disaster, flood or famine, and those who work to relieve suffering in any way.
We pray for those who work to bring peace and unity to areas of strife.

We pray for all who are suffering from hunger or disruption in their lives and relationships.
We ask your blessing upon all who are ill and we pray to you for those whom we know . . .
Almighty and powerful God,
be our strength and our help.

God of all, we thank you for Willibrord and those who left this land to take the Good News to others.
We rejoice in the communion of saints and our loved ones departed, and we pray especially for . . .
Merciful Father,
accept these prayers for the sake of your Son, our Saviour, Jesus Christ.
Amen.

The peace

The joy of the Lord be your strength.
The love of the Lord warm your life.
The peace of the Lord be in all your actions.
The peace of the Lord be always with you.
And also with you.

Blessing

God give you his light to guide you,
his love to enfold you,
his strength to encourage you:
and the blessing of God Almighty, the Father, the Son and the Holy Spirit, be upon you and remain with you always.
Amen.

8 NOVEMBER

Saints and Martyrs of England/of Wales

Today the churches in England and Wales celebrate the rich heritage of the saints who have helped to build up the Church in these lands. Holy men and women, martyrs for the faith, those who brought the gospel to our country, and those who suffered during the Reformation. We remember also the holy men and women who have no memorial but this day, yet helped to forward the faith and to build up the Church in their days. We remember how we have been enriched by peoples of other nations, cultures and traditions in the growing of the Church and the spreading of the gospel: and we rejoice in the communion of saints.

Readings

Isaiah 61:4-9
Revelation 19:5-10
John 17:18-23

Opening prayer

Blessed are you, Lord our God, for you have raised up among us saints to witness to your presence, your love, and compassion for all. Grant that by their dedication we may be inspired to give ourselves more fully in your service and reveal your love and peace in the way we live: we ask this in the love of Christ, our Lord.

Intercessions

God, as you call us, make us worthy of our calling.
We remember those who have shone like lights in the darkness of the world and those who are doing the same today.
We ask your blessing upon all who are growing in the faith and on those seeking to live a holy life: we pray for their guides and teachers.

We ask your blessing upon all who administer the sacraments and those who preach the Word: we pray for the clergy of our area.
Lord, may we be faithful witnesses to you in our daily lives.
By the lives of your saints,
inspire us, good Lord.

God, as you call us, help us to live purposeful lives and work for the wellbeing of all creation.
We pray for all who are called to positions of authority and we pray for Elizabeth our Queen.
We ask your blessing upon those who shape our lives by the decisions they make, in government and in industry.
We pray for all who work in the media and influence our ways of thinking, that they may act with responsibility and care.
By the lives of your saints,
inspire us, good Lord.

God, as you call us, we ask your blessing upon those who have inspired us by their lives, their example and dedication to their calling.
We pray for those who give their time and talent to the building up of our community and the world around them.
We pray for those who teach our young, that they may inspire and open eyes to the wonders of our world.
We ask your blessing upon our loved ones, our families, and our friends.
By the lives of your saints,
inspire us, good Lord.

God, as you call us, may we all share in the healing of the world and in the working for peace.
We remember all who are persecuted for their faith, those who have lost their work or their homes: may we help where we can.
We pray for all who are ill or struggling with infirmities, for their carers and loved ones.
We pray for those whom we know who are in illness or need . . .
By the lives of your saints,
inspire us, good Lord.

God, as you call us, we give you thanks for the saints of this land who served you faithfully and are now in the glory of your kingdom. May our loved ones departed be one with them in the communion of saints: and we now remember them before you . . .
Merciful Father,
accept these prayers for the sake of your Son, our Saviour, Jesus Christ.
Amen.

The peace

God, who has called you into life,
to his love and peace,
make you to be numbered with his saints.
The peace of the Lord be always with you.
And also with you.

Blessing

God, who loves you with an everlasting love,
encourage and strengthen you in your faith,
give you a firm hope in him,
and, as with his saints, empower you to reveal his love:
and the blessing of God Almighty, the Father, the Son and the Holy Spirit, be upon you and remain with you always.
Amen.

10 NOVEMBER

Leo the Great

There is no record of the early life of Leo, though it is believed he was born in Rome of Tuscan parents. He was a deacon at Rome and was important enough to correspond with Cyril of Alexandria, and John Cassian dedicated a treatise on the Incarnation to him. He was elected Pope in 440 and served as Pope for 20 years. His statement on the Incarnation of Christ was acclaimed by the Council of Chalcedon in 451 as the official teaching of the Church. Many believe this statement to be one of the early highlights in Christian history. He sought to free Rome from the barbarians and to restore the spiritual and material damage that had been caused. After Attila the Hun had sacked Milan he moved against Rome. Pope Leo met him and persuaded him to accept tribute rather than sack Rome. Later the Vandal Genseric came with a large army; again Leo sought to free Rome from plundering, but the city was plundered for 14 days. His writings and actions show Leo's strong belief in the primacy of Rome. He died in 461.

Readings

Ecclesiasticus 39:6-10
1 Peter 5:1-11
Matthew 16:13-19

Opening prayer

God of all, we give you thanks and praise for the life of Leo the Great, defender of the faith and a Doctor of the Church, and remember how he protected the city of Rome against invasion. May we be strengthened by you to stand firm in our faith and against the evils of our time: we ask this in the name of Christ, our Lord.

Intercessions

God of grace, may the Church always be ready to use its resources for the good of the people.
May the churches be good stewards of what they have received.
We pray for Pope Francis, the Church in Rome and for the Roman Catholic Church throughout the world.
We remember areas where the Church is oppressed and persecuted and pray that the people remain faithful in their troubles.
Loving Lord,
hear us and guide us.

God of grace, we ask your blessing upon all who work in conservation and the protection of the environment.
We pray for those who seek to preserve endangered species and the ancient forests of our world.
We ask your guidance upon all who produce our food, that the land is not overworked and that wild life is given space and respect.
May we be aware of our stewardship in the use of the world's resources.
Loving Lord,
hear us and guide us.

God of grace, we pray that our homes may not be wasteful or careless in the use of what we have.
We remember all who are made homeless, who suffer from hunger, or lack proper care.
We pray for those with few resources and for the work of Fair Trade and the relief organisations.
We ask your blessing upon our homes, schools and the communities to which we belong.
Loving Lord,
hear us and guide us.

God of grace, we give thanks for all who work to protect others and pray for all Safe Houses and children's homes.
We pray for all who have suffered from violence or abuse, for their healing and restoring to wellbeing.

We remember those who have been involved in accidents and ask your blessing upon the police and emergency services.
We pray for all who are ill, and remember before you, O Lord, friends and loved ones in their troubles . . .
Loving Lord,
hear us and guide us.

God of grace, we give thanks for life and life eternal.
We pray for friends and loved ones departed from us . . .
Merciful Father,
accept these prayers for the sake of your Son, our Saviour, Jesus Christ.
Amen.

The peace

The Lord, who is the source of peace,
give you peace at all times and in all places,
and make you an instrument of his peace.
The peace of the Lord be always with you.
And also with you.

Blessing

God, who loves you with an everlasting love,
give you a firm trust in him,
encourage and strengthen you in the faith,
empower you to reveal his love:
and the blessing of God Almighty, the Father, the Son and the Holy Spirit, be upon you and remain with you always.
Amen.

11 NOVEMBER

Martin of Tours

Martin was born about the year 316 in Sabaria in Pannonia, now Hungary. He was the son of a pagan officer in the Roman army and expected to follow his father's career. It was probably as a conscript that he was called up. Before this, at the age of ten, he had shown an interest in becoming a Christian, much to his father's dismay. He became a catechumen while a soldier. One cold winter's night while at Amiens he was out wearing his cloak when he met an almost naked beggar: he had nothing to give him, so he cut his cloak in half and gave half to the beggar. That night he had a dream, and he saw Christ with the saints. Christ had Martin's half-cloak and said, 'Look what Martin, while still a catechumen, has clothed me with today.' As a Christian, he felt he could no longer serve in the army and tried to end his military career at 40. He was imprisoned for this for a day but afterwards released from the army. Martin became a disciple of Bishop Hilary of Poitiers. He then decided to become a hermit. Soon others joined him in what was to be the first monastery in all of Gaul. In 372 he was consecrated as Bishop of Tours. He continued to live the simple life of a monk, travelling on foot or on a donkey. He lived in a monastic cell near the cathedral. As he gained more followers he moved his monastery to Marmoutier. He saw the monastic life as a way of reaching rural areas in outreach and care. Martin's army discipline served him well: through it he brought order and obedience to his community. Like soldiers they travelled lightly and only ate one meal a day. Martin died in 397 and was buried at Tours.

Readings

Isaiah 61:1-3
1 Thessalonians 5:1-11
Matthew 25:34-40

Opening prayer

God, who called Martin from serving in the Roman army to be a soldier of Christ, may we learn from his example and seek to see Christ in others and bring Christ to others: we ask this in the love of our Saviour, Jesus Christ.

Intercessions

Ever loving God, as we give thanks for Martin, we ask your blessing upon the Church in France and the diocese of Tours.
We pray for all who serve you in their caring for others and in being generous to the needy.
May we discover where we can be of service to Christ in the needs of the world and where we can reveal his love for all.
May we look upon the world with the love you have for it, and bring to those we meet an awareness of your love and presence with them.
Ever present God,
hear us and help us.

Ever loving God, we pray for the people of France and for all who seek to keep peace and unity within their country.
We pray for those who seek to bring healing to divided communities and nations.
We remember all who have objected to war as a means of solving the problems and animosity between nations: we remember those who suffered for objecting and for their families.
May we seek to bring peace, harmony and justice to the communities to which we belong.
Ever present God,
hear us and help us.

Ever loving God, we give thanks for your abiding presence in our lives and homes, and we ask your blessing upon all our loved ones.
We pray for homes where young people have to work to make ends meet and often have to give up on hopes of further education.
We pray for families who have welcomed a new birth and for the care they receive from the district nurses.

We remember those who live alone, especially if they are not coping well, and ask your blessing upon their helpers.
Ever present God,
hear us and help us.

Ever loving God, as we remember Martin, we pray for the homeless and for those who live on the streets.
We pray for all who work to relieve poverty, homelessness and hunger within our world.
We pray for those who struggle with their fears, anxieties and bad memories.
We ask your blessing upon all who are ill or troubled, and we pray for those known to us . . .
Ever present God,
hear us and help us.

Ever loving God, as we give thanks for Martin, we rejoice in the communion of saints.
We remember in your presence our loved ones departed . . .
Merciful Father,
accept these prayers for the sake of your Son, our Saviour, Jesus Christ.
Amen.

The peace

Let the love of Christ dwell in your hearts
and the peace of Christ in your actions.
The peace of the Lord be always with you.
And also with you.

Blessing

Abide in God's presence,
abide in his love,
abide in his peace,
abide in his light:
and the blessing of God Almighty, the Father, the Son and the Holy Spirit, be upon you and remain with you always.
Amen.

13 NOVEMBER

Charles Simeon

Charles Simeon was born in 1759 at Reading. As a young man he was an evangelical. While preparing to go to college, he became deeply aware of the redeeming love of God. He looked back on this as a turning point in his life. He was educated at Cambridge University and spent the rest of his life in that city. He became a fellow of King's College in 1782 and was ordained priest the following year. He became vicar of Holy Trinity church in the city. Because he had been appointed through his family connections, many of his parishioners did not readily welcome him. But his pastoral care, his love for all and his preaching not only won them round but soon increased the congregation. Inside the pulpit of the church he had carved the words from St John's Gospel: 'Sir, we would see Jesus.' This was to ever remind him that people came not for the skill of the preacher but for their need to know Jesus. As one of the leading evangelicals, he had a large influence on the Church. He was also one of the founders of the Church Missionary Society. He set up the Simeon Trust which made appointments to parishes of fellow evangelicals. He was still the vicar of Holy Trinity when he died in 1836.

Readings

Malachi 2:5-7
Colossians 1:3-8
Luke 8:4-8

Opening prayer

Gracious God, we give you thanks and praise for the life of Charles Simeon, his pastoral ministry and his outreach to others. As he used his talents to the good of many and to your glory, may we use the gifts you have given us to your praise and glory: we ask this in the love of Jesus Christ, our Lord.

Intercessions

Good Shepherd, we give you thanks for the faithful service of Charles Simeon in his pastoral ministry, and pray for Holy Trinity church, Cambridge.
We ask your blessing upon the Church Missionary Society and on all who are concerned with the outreach of your Church.
We give thanks for the work of the Simeon Trust and ask your blessing upon all priests and pastors.
Lord, may we share in the pastoral ministry and encourage others to see and love Jesus.
Lord, open our eyes to your presence,
and our hearts to your love.

Good Shepherd, we pray for all who act as carers and those who seek out the lost and the needy.
We remember those who are teaching their skills to others and for all who are learning a trade.
We ask your blessing on all universities, colleges and schools and on those who influence the minds of others.
We pray for our government and all who are in positions of authority throughout the world.
Lord, open our eyes to your presence,
and our hearts to your love.

Good Shepherd, we pray that within our communities our eyes may be opened to new people and new ideas.
We ask that, in our homes and lives, we may be seen as those who love you and all of your creation.
We pray that we may reveal your love and compassion by the way we care for the people around us.
May we know we serve you in caring for others and meet you in our meeting with others.
Lord, open our eyes to your presence,
and our hearts to your love.

Good Shepherd, you seek out the straying and the lost; we ask your blessing upon all who care for the ill, the lonely and the needy.
We pray for any who are distress or in trouble and feel they have no helpers.

We remember the world's poor, the war-torn, and the refugees: may we help where we can and show our compassion to all.
We pray for all who are ill, and we remember those known to us . . .
Lord, open our eyes to your presence,
and our hearts to your love.

Good Shepherd, calling us to your love and to eternal life, we give thanks for Charles Simeon and his witness for you.
We pray for all the faithful departed and remember our friends and loved ones who are now in the fullness of your kingdom . . .
Merciful Father,
accept these prayers for the sake of your Son, our Saviour, Jesus Christ. Amen.

The peace

The peace of God, the Creator, be upon you.
The peace of Christ, the Prince of Peace, be about you.
The peace of the Holy Spirit be within you.
The peace of the Lord be always with you.
And also with you.

Blessing

God, the Creator, shepherd and shield you;
Christ, the Light of the World, lighten your life;
the Holy Spirit of God inspire and guide you:
and the blessing of God Almighty, the Father, the Son and the Holy Spirit, be upon you and remain with you always.
Amen.

16 NOVEMBER

Margaret, Queen of Scotland

Margaret was born in 1046, the daughter of Edward the Exile and the granddaughter of Edmund Ironside. She received her education mostly in Hungary where her family had gone into exile. After the Norman Conquest in 1066 she was among the last of the Anglo-Saxon royal family. She fled to safety in Scotland under the protection of Malcolm III, King of Scotland, whom she married in 1069. Margaret was active in her faith. She shared in the reforming of the Church in Scotland, and in the foundation of monasteries and hostels for pilgrims. She saw to the renewing of the abbey at Iona. Her life was noted for her regular prayer life, spiritual reading, lavish almsgiving and her church needlework. Among her buildings, she caused the abbey at Dunfermline to be built, as the Scottish equivalent of Westminster. When she died in 1093, she was buried in Dunfermline beside her husband.

Readings

Proverbs 31:10-12, 20, 26-31
1 Corinthians 12:13–13:3
Matthew 25:34-40

Opening prayer

O Lord of love, we give you thanks for the love of Queen Margaret for the poor, and for her support for the churches, monasteries and pilgrims' hostels. May we be generous in our support of others and seek to reveal your love for all: we ask this in the name of our Lord Jesus Christ.

Intercessions

Holy and eternal God, we give you thanks for Queen Margaret and pray for the Church in Scotland, its places of pilgrimage and monasteries.

We ask your blessing upon the Church in Iona and the Iona Community, for Dunfermline Abbey and the people of Dunfermline.
We pray for all who go on pilgrimage to holy places, and for those seeking to know you.
We pray for the Children's Society and the work of the Church among young people.
Holy and Strong One,
hear us and help us.

Holy and eternal God, we pray for the people of Scotland, for the Scottish Parliament and its leaders.
We pray for all who seek to uphold Scottish traditions, culture and music.
We remember all who work on the oil rigs, those who provide us with fuel.
We ask your blessing upon Elizabeth our Queen and all the royal family.
Holy and Strong One,
hear us and help us.

Holy and eternal God, we give thanks for all who have been benefactors to our community life and pray that we may contribute to the community and its organisations.
We ask your blessing upon those who lead the local organisations and on our local councils.
We pray for all who maintain the parks and gardens, those who keep our streets clean and the collectors of our refuse.
We pray for our loved ones, for our friends and for our neighbours.
Holy and Strong One,
hear us and help us.

Holy and eternal God, we pray for all who seek to bring aid to those in trouble.
We remember the work of the emergency services and pray for ambulance workers and those in the fire brigade.
We remember those in need and pray for the work of food banks and the social services.

We ask your blessing upon the sick and the suffering, and name before you those for whom we are concerned . . .
Holy and Strong One,
hear us and help us.

Holy and eternal God, we give thanks for the life and generosity of Queen Margaret and pray for all your saints in glory.
We remember those who have died this week and those that are bereaved.
We pray for all the departed and remember especially those in our hearts . . .
Merciful Father,
accept these prayers for the sake of your Son, our Saviour, Jesus Christ. Amen.

The peace

Walk in the light of the Lord
and the paths of peace:
The peace of the Lord be always with you.
And also with you.

Blessing

Trust in the compassion of God,
abide in his unfailing love,
rejoice in his saving power:
and the blessing of God Almighty, the Father, the Son and the Holy Spirit, be upon you and remain with you always.
Amen.

17 NOVEMBER

Hugh of Lincoln

Hugh was born about 1140 at Avalon, near Grenoble in Burgundy. He was educated by the Augustinian Canons and made his profession with them. At the age of 25, he left them to become a monk at the Grande Chartreuse. Then he was invited by Henry II to become the Prior of a failing Carthusian monastery at Witham, Somerset. Under Hugh the monastery flourished and grew in number. In 1186 Hugh was consecrated as Bishop of Lincoln, the largest diocese in England. Hugh immediately set about bringing new vigour and order to the cathedral and diocese: he organised synods and his visitations throughout the large area. He embarked on repairs to the cathedral which had been damaged by an earthquake, enlarging it at the same time. He revived the Lincoln schools. He set about caring for the ill, the poor and the oppressed, including concern for the Jews and for lepers. In the process of doing this, he challenged other bishops and lords. He was regarded as one of the great leaders of the Church and died in 1200.

Readings

Ezekiel 3:16-21
1 Timothy 6:11-16
John 15:9-17

Opening prayer

Almighty God, we rejoice this day in the life of Hugh, his strengthening the Church, reforming the Carthusian monastery at Witham, and bringing new energy and life to the cathedral at Lincoln. Following his example, may we endeavour to be generous in the care of all who are in need: we ask this in the name of our Saviour, Jesus Christ.

Intercessions

God of grace, as we give thanks for Hugh, we pray for the diocese and people of Lincoln.
We ask your blessing upon those who work among people with leprosy and pray for the Leprosy Mission.
We ask your blessing upon those who work among the outcasts of society and seek to give them some dignity in themselves.
We pray for a sense of outreach and mission, that we may show the love and joy of the gospel in our daily lives.
Lord of love and mercy,
help us and guide us.

God of grace, we pray for the World Health Organisation and all who give their lives to relieve suffering throughout the world.
We pray for those who work for the healing of the nations, to bring peace, unity and harmony to all.
We ask your blessing upon world leaders and all who are in control of the resources of the world.
We pray for those whose harvest has failed, that they may receive aid and help from the world community.
Lord of love and mercy,
help us and guide us.

God of grace, we pray for all separated from loved ones, through illness, war, or any circumstance.
We pray for all who are lonely or not coping well on their own.
We pray for homes where there is violence, or a breakdown in relationships.
We ask your blessing upon our homes, loved ones and families, and thank you for all the love we share.
Lord of love and mercy,
help us and guide us.

God of grace, we pray for all who suffer from leprosy or physical disfigurement.
We pray for minority groups that are being oppressed and pray for justice and freedom for all people.
We ask your blessing upon all who work within the National Health

Service and upon our local doctors and nurses.
We pray for all who are ill at this time, and remember before you those for whom we ought to pray . . .
Lord of love and mercy,
help us and guide us.

God of grace, we give thanks for the talents of Hugh, his work at Lincoln and for all your saints in glory.
We pray for our loved ones and friends departed, asking that they may rejoice in your love and peace . . .
Merciful Father,
accept these prayers for the sake of your Son, our Saviour, Jesus Christ.
Amen.

The peace

The peace of God the creator surrounds you.
The peace of Christ our Lord enfolds you.
The peace of the powerful Spirit is within you.
The peace of the Lord be always with you.
And also with you.

Blessing

The Almighty God be your strength,
Christ the Lord be your Saviour,
the Spirit of God be your guide:
and the blessing of God Almighty, the Father, the Son and the Holy Spirit, be upon you and remain with you always.
Amen.

18 NOVEMBER

Elizabeth of Hungary

Elizabeth was born in 1207, the daughter of King Andrew II of Hungary. She was given in marriage to Louis IV of Thuringia, with whom she had three children. But after only four years Louis died and Elizabeth was cast out of the court and castle by her brother-in-law. She settled in Marburg and in time became a Franciscan tertiary. She spent much of her time caring for the poor, even fishing, cooking and cleaning for them. Her special care was for the children in a hospital where she especially looked after the deformed and the dirtiest of children: the children started calling her 'Mother'. But due to the hard life she was living, she died in 1231 at the age of 24.

Readings

Proverbs 31:10-end
1 John 3:14-18
Matthew 25:31-end

Opening prayer

Holy God, who strengthened Elizabeth of Hungary to serve Christ in the care of the poor and amid all her troubles to remain firm in her faith, help us also to be strong in our faith and to serve Christ in the care of others: in your grace and goodness we ask this in the name of Jesus Christ, our Lord.

Intercessions

God of love and compassion, as we give thanks for Elizabeth of Hungary, we ask your blessing upon the Church and its care for children.
We pray for church schools, Sunday schools, confirmation classes, and Religious Education.

We pray for the work of the Children's Society and for all who support it.
We ask your blessing upon the Franciscans and pray especially today for the Third Order of the Franciscans.
Loving Lord,
help us as we call upon you.

God of love and compassion, we give you thanks for all who show your love and care in the way they look after others.
We ask your blessing upon those who work among the poor and the outcasts of society.
We pray for the Probation Service and all who look after young offenders.
We pray for those who foster and those who have adopted children.
Loving Lord,
help us as we call upon you.

God of love and compassion, bless our homes, and all our relationships: may we never take one another for granted.
May we treat everyone we meet with the respect that we would pay to Christ our Lord.
We pray for all who are locked in themselves, through self-centredness, selfishness and greed.
May we, through our love for creation, reveal your love in the world.
Loving Lord,
help us as we call upon you.

God of love and compassion, we ask that in all our struggles and sorrows we may know your presence and love.
We pray for all who feel unloved and rejected, or that their lives are being wasted.
We remember those who struggle with depression, and those who live in darkness or fear.
We ask your blessing upon all who are ill or distressed in any way: and we remember before you friends and loved ones in their suffering . . .
Merciful Father,
accept these prayers for the sake of your Son, our Saviour, Jesus Christ. Amen.

The peace

Accept God's peace.
Let God's peace dwell in your heart.
Show his peace, and share his peace.
The peace of the Lord be always with you.
And also with you.

Blessing

The power of God protect you,
the grace of God go with you,
the goodness of God guide you:
and the blessing of God Almighty, the Father, the Son and the Holy Spirit, be upon you and remain with you always.
Amen.

19 NOVEMBER

Hilda of Whitby

Hilda was born in 614 in the area of Elmet, which is near Leeds in North Yorkshire. She was related to the royal family of Northumbria. When her father was poisoned, she came under the protection of King Edwin. When Edwin was baptised in York, she was also baptised by Paulinus at the age of 12. The first half of her life she lived a secular life of which little is known. At the age of 33 she decided to become a nun at Chelles, near Paris. However, Aidan of Lindisfarne persuaded her to be a nun in Northumbria and gave her a parcel of land on the north bank of the river Wear. After a while, she moved from there to an established monastery at Hartlepool, to be the Abbess. There she organised the monastery along the lines of the Irish Church. In 657 she went to Whitby to re-establish or to found the double monastery for both men and women. Soon Whitby became famous for its learning and its library: it trained at least five bishops. Here in 664, the Synod of Whitby took place. Though Hilda supported the Irish party, she accepted the decision in favour of the Church of Rome. In 678 she supported Archbishop Theodore in the division of the large diocese of Northumbria. Two of her former students became bishops of a new diocese in this action. Hilda also supported the translation of Bible stories into the vernacular through her encouraging of Caedmon the cowherd to produce poetry in the Anglo-Saxon language. For the last years of her life, Hilda suffered from chronic illness; she died in 680.

Readings

Isaiah 61:10–62:5
Acts 4:32-35
Luke 12:32-37

Opening prayer

Creator of light and love, we give you thanks for Hilda, who shone as a bright light in the Dark Ages. As she worked for the unity of a divided Church, we pray that we may work for unity and peace in both the Church and the world: we ask this in the name of the Prince of Peace, Jesus Christ our Lord.

Intercessions

Lord of light, as we give thanks for Hilda, we pray for the church of St Hilda's Hartlepool, for the churches in Whitby and for the diocese of York.
We ask your blessing upon the community of the Holy Paraclete at Whitby and upon all religious communities.
We pray for all members of church synods and councils, and for all who make decisions concerning the outreach and unity of the Church.
We pray for those who teach, preach and inspire others through the Scriptures.
Lighten our darkness,
Lord, we pray.

Lord of light, we give thanks and pray for all who encourage the arts, and pray for artists, musicians, craftspeople, poets, and story-tellers.
We pray for all who brighten our world through their example and dedication, and pray for architects, builders and those who care for parks and gardens.
May we remember that the world is yours and care for it with respect and compassion towards all creatures.
We ask your blessing upon all research scientists, inventors, and those who seek to provide food for all of humankind.
Lighten our darkness,
Lord, we pray.

Lord of light, we give thanks for all who have loved us, guided us and protected us and we ask your blessing upon our homes and families.
We pray for children who have been orphaned or lost a parent through war or violence and for all single parents.
We remember all who foster children and those who adopt them.
We pray for the Children's Society and for all homes and places of care for children in need.
Lighten our darkness,
Lord, we pray.

Lord of light, we remember before you the troubles and perils of people and nations.
We remember the needs of refugees and all who are without helpers, those who have lost hope and the starving.
We ask your blessing upon the world-weary and those whose abilities and powers are failing.
We pray for all who are ill or suffering in any way, and remember in your presence those for whom we ought to pray . . .
Lighten our darkness,
Lord, we pray.

Lord of light and giver of life eternal, we give you thanks for the wisdom and dedication of Hilda and we rejoice in the fellowship of your saints in glory.
We pray for all the departed, and especially for those dear to us . . .
Merciful Father,
accept these prayers for the sake of your Son, our Saviour, Jesus Christ.
Amen.

The peace

Grace, mercy and peace be upon you and your loved ones from God who loves you with an everlasting love.
The peace of the Lord be always with you.
And also with you.

Blessing

The Lord look upon you with his steadfast love;
God, your Creator, give you of his strength;
God, your Saviour, rescue you from darkness;
God, the Holy Spirit, fill you with newness of life:
and the blessing of God Almighty, the Father, the Son and the Holy Spirit, be upon you and remain with you always.
Amen.

20 NOVEMBER

Edmund, King of the East Angles

Edmund was born around the year 840. So he was very young when he was crowned king of Norfolk in 855, and king of Suffolk in 856. As king, he made great efforts to suppress lawlessness, and to care for and protect the poor. In 869–870 the Great Army of the Vikings under Ingwar invaded East Anglia. Edmund led an army against them but he was defeated and captured. Edmund refused to renounce his faith or his right to rule. After scourging him to get him to change his mind, the Vikings tied him to a tree and shot arrows at him. They finally beheaded him at Hellesdon, Norfolk, in 870. His body was buried in a small wooden chapel nearby. In about 915 his body was transferred to Bedriesworth, which is now known as Bury St Edmunds.

Readings

Proverbs 20:28; 21:1-4, 7
Hebrews 11:32-40
John 12:24-26

Opening prayer

God of grace, we give you thanks for Edmund, king of the East Angles, remembering his courage in facing the foe and concern for his people, and ask that you will help us to be steadfast in the faith and with courage witness to your love: we ask this in the name of Christ, who gave himself for us.

Intercessions

Good and gracious God, we ask your blessing upon the Church in Norfolk and Suffolk and on all who live within that area.
We pray for all those who are being persecuted for their faith, and those who face torture, prison, scorn and rejection.

We pray for Christians who get no support from their family or friends in their desire to serve you.
In the midst of troubles, may we witness to your love and to the peace you give.
Lord of compassion and mercy,
deliver us from evil.

Good and gracious God, we ask your blessing upon Elizabeth our Queen and upon all the royal family.
We pray for rulers of people and nations, that they may seek to be instruments of unity and peace.
We pray for all in positions of authority, that they may not misuse their powers but work with compassion and integrity.
We pray for prison visitors and for the work of Amnesty International.
Lord of compassion and mercy,
deliver us from evil.

Good and gracious God, we give thanks for the freedom and peace which we have and pray we may use it aright.
We remember all who are restricted due to harsh laws and despotic rule.
We remember families separated through war or violence and who are in search of their loved ones.
We ask your blessing upon our homes, loved ones and the communities to which we belong.
Lord of compassion and mercy,
deliver us from evil.

Good and gracious God, we remember all who offer their lives in the care of others, especially those working in dangerous places.
We pray for the Red Cross and all relief workers.
We ask your blessing upon all medical research workers who are seeking cures for the diseases and troubles of our world, and we pray for the World Health Organisation.
We pray for all who are ill or in difficulty at this time and remember friends and loved ones in their illness or needs . . .
Lord of compassion and mercy,
deliver us from evil.

Good and gracious God, we give you thanks for King Edmund and all who witness to their faith in your love and life eternal.
We pray for all our loved ones departed from us, remembering especially . . .
Merciful Father,
accept these prayers for the sake of your Son, our Saviour, Jesus Christ.
Amen.

The peace

The presence of God,
the power of God,
the peace of God,
be around you and within you.
The peace of the Lord be always with you.
And also with you.

Blessing

God, the Creator, protect you from evil;
Christ, the Saviour, be your light in the darkness;
the Spirit of God be your strength and guide you:
and the blessing of God Almighty, the Father, the Son and the Holy Spirit, be upon you and remain with you always.
Amen.

23 NOVEMBER

Clement of Rome

Clement was a Roman citizen and a Jew by birth. Tradition has it he was converted to Christianity by the disciples of St Peter and St Paul. He was probably the third successor after Peter as Bishop of Rome. Clement is best known for his Epistle to the Corinthians written about the year 96. This gives an insight into the Bishop of Rome seeking to intervene in the affairs of another church. It also provides the earliest evidence for the residence and martyrdom of Peter and Paul in Rome. Clement is thought to have been an early martyr. A fourth-century account of his life suggests he was exiled to Crimea and compelled to work in the salt mines. He was said to have been killed later by being thrown into the sea with an anchor around his neck about the year 100.

Readings

Jeremiah 1:4-10
Philippians 3:17–4:3
Matthew 16:13-19

Opening prayer

Lord of all power and might, we give you thanks for the early Church and remember Clement as Bishop of Rome at a time when it was dangerous for people to declare they were Christians. May we be bold in our faith and steadfast in our love of you: we ask this in the name of Jesus Christ, our Lord.

Intercessions

Lord of all creation, we pray for the Church in Rome and throughout Italy.
We ask your blessing upon Pope Francis and his attempts at reform and his reaching out in mission.

We give thanks for the diversity of the Church and pray we may also show its unity in faith.
We ask your blessing upon our bishop . . . and upon all who have pastoral care for us.
God, in your grace and goodness,
guide us and help us.

Lord of all creation, we remember those who are in prison because of their stand against injustice or violence, and those unjustly imprisoned without reason.
We pray for those who are humiliated and those who are tortured.
We remember those who have just disappeared and those who feel they are forgotten.
We ask your blessing upon their loved ones and especially if they are also in danger.
God, in your grace and goodness,
guide us and help us.

Lord of all creation, we ask for your guidance and strength in our daily lives, that we may stand for the truth and witness to your love.
We pray for young people growing up in a world with so many calls upon their attention, and so much that can lead them astray.
We remember all who are led astray and who have lost trust and faith in others.
We ask your blessing upon our families, our friends and loved ones, that they may live in love, peace and freedom.
God, in your grace and goodness,
guide us and help us.

Lord of all creation, we pray for those who are troubled or confused and for their carers and loved ones.
We remember all who live alone and are struggling in any way.
We ask your blessing upon all who are in hospital or a hospice and for those who are looking after them.
We pray for all who are ill and remember friends and loved ones who are suffering in any way . . .
God, in your grace and goodness,
guide us and help us.

Lord of all creation, we give you thanks for the gift of life and for life eternal.
We pray for Clement and for all the faithful departed, and we remember friends and loved ones in your eternal kingdom . . .
Merciful Father,
accept these prayers for the sake of your Son, our Saviour, Jesus Christ. Amen.

The peace

God, in his goodness, guide you into the ways of unity and peace and that you may live in harmony with all of creation.
The peace of the Lord be always with you.
And also with you.

Blessing

God, who created you and called you to know and love him,
guide, strengthen, protect you
and keep you in his peace:
and the blessing of God Almighty, the Father, the Son and the Holy Spirit, be upon you and remain with you always.
Amen.

DECEMBER

6 DECEMBER

Nicholas

Nicholas was Bishop of Myra, in south-west Turkey in the fourth century. He may have attended the Council of Nicaea which opposed the Arian heresy. Otherwise, little is known of his life. In the ninth century, a hagiography enhanced his reputation as a wonder worker and a person of great generosity. It showed Nicholas as caring for children, feeding the hungry and healing the sick. One story tells of how he saved three young sisters from a life of prostitution by providing them with dowries. With this and his gifts to children, he became the patron saint of children. Because of his gifts of three bags of gold, he became the patron saint of pawnbrokers, and their sign throughout many centuries was three golden balls. He is also patron saint of Russia and of sailors. Due to his gifts to children, it became a tradition to give children gifts on this day and he was therefore the inspiration for Santa Claus.

Readings

Isaiah 61:1-3
1 Timothy 6:6-11
Mark 10:13-16

Opening prayer

We give thanks for the generosity of Nicholas and his compassion for those in need. We pray that we may never fail to be generous to those in need; as we have received much, teach us to give without stint: we ask this in the name of Jesus, who gave himself for us.

Intercessions

Generous God, we ask your blessing upon the Church in Turkey and in Russia; we pray for areas where it is difficult to be a Christian or to share in worship.

We pray for the Mission to Seafarers, for their places of safety and for their care of those whose work is upon the sea.
We remember areas of poverty where the Church is constantly at work, and pray for Christian Aid, CAFOD and all relief workers.
Lord, giver of all good things,
hear our prayers.

Generous God, we ask your blessing upon those who work with children in need.
We pray for the street children of our world, those who live in squalid rooms and those who sleep rough.
We remember those who are abused, or forced into prostitution due to their poverty.
We pray for the Children's Society and for the Save the Children Fund.
Lord, giver of all good things,
hear our prayers.

Generous God, as we give thanks for our homes, we pray for those who live in shanty towns and refugee camps where there is inadequate sanitation and little or no fresh water.
We remember families squeezed into a small space and where there is no privacy, and those with no place to call home.
We give thanks for all who supply us with food, water, light and care, and pray that we may remember those who lack any of these.
We ask your blessing upon our loved ones and our community, and pray for their wellbeing and safety.
Lord, giver of all good things,
hear our prayers.

Generous God, we give thanks for our Health Service and pray for all who lack proper medical care.
We pray for mothers giving birth in surroundings that endanger their health and the health of their children.
We pray for all who are deprived or suffering in any way.
We pray for all who are ill at home or in hospital, and we remember before you those for whom we ought to pray . . .
Lord, giver of all good things,
hear our prayers.

Generous God, we give thanks for Nicholas and his example of care and action.
We pray for all who are departed, that they may rejoice in the fellowship of the saints in glory.
We pray for our own loved ones who have died and remember them before you . . .
Merciful Father,
accept these prayers for the sake of your Son, our Saviour, Jesus Christ.
Amen.

The peace

God's presence and peace be in your hearts and homes,
in your going out and coming in,
in your actions and in your rest.
The peace of the Lord be always with you.
And also with you.

Blessing

God be with you on every road,
guide your every step,
protect you in the storms,
enfold you in his peace:
and the blessing of God Almighty, the Father, the Son and the Holy Spirit, be upon you and remain with you always.
Amen.

7 DECEMBER

Ambrose of Milan

Ambrose was born in 339 at Trier, now in Germany but then the capital of the prefecture of Gaul. Ambrose's father was the Praetorian prefect. As a young man, Ambrose worked as a lawyer. In 370 he was appointed governor of Liguria and Aemilia with his residence in Milan. In 374, much to his amazement, by popular acclaim he was appointed Bishop of Milan. At this stage, though a catechumen, he was not baptised. He was baptised and his consecration soon followed. He proved an outstanding bishop, who was not afraid to challenge the emperor or to stand firm against Arianism. St Augustine came under his influence; he was partly responsible for Augustine's conversion, and baptised him in Milan Cathedral in 386. It was said that Ambrose was so popular because he tried to be accessible to all who sought him for guidance or help. He died in 397.

Readings

Isaiah 41:9b-13
Ephesians 3:8-13
Luke 22:24-30

Opening prayer

Lord, as Ambrose heard your call in the voice of the people, may we be sensitive to your call through others and to hear your voice in the needs of the people and in your creation, and so work with you for the good of all: we ask this in the name of Jesus Christ, our Lord.

Intercessions

God most holy, as you called Ambrose to be a bishop, a teacher of the faith and a man of courage, give to your Church men and women of courage who will speak boldly for the faith.

We ask your blessing upon the Church in Milan and upon all the people of Italy.
We pray for the Church where there is opposition to its teaching and for Christians whose lives are endangered.
We give thanks for all poets and hymn writers, and ask your blessing upon church musicians, organists and the writers of music for worship.
Holy God, Holy and Strong One,
be our hope and our strength in trouble.

God most holy, we ask your blessing upon all who have the courage to speak out against the misuse of power or resources.
We remember all who have lost their work or position through standing for justice and integrity of actions.
We pray for Elizabeth our Queen, for Parliament and for all leaders of industry.
We ask your blessing upon those who work to protect minorities that are being oppressed and for their safety.
Holy God, Holy and Strong One,
be our hope and our strength in trouble.

God most holy, we pray for our communities, that they may be places of compassion and sensitivity, and that they may hear the call of those in need.
We pray for all who are suffering from poverty or homelessness, or who feel rejected by society.
We give you thanks for our homes and our loved ones, and ask your blessing upon us.
Lord, as we have richly received, may we, with joy, care for any who are in need or difficulty.
Holy God, Holy and Strong One,
be our hope and our strength in trouble.

God most holy, we ask your blessing upon all who are afraid as their abilities and powers wane.
We pray for all who are disabled and for those who cannot cope on their own.
We remember all struggling with ill health, and pray for their loved ones and friends who are their support and comfort.

We remember all who are ill or suffering and we pray for those who are known to us . . .
Holy God, Holy and Strong One,
be our hope and our strength in trouble.

God most holy, you have called us into life and an awareness of you: may we live to your glory and praise.
We give you thanks for Ambrose, for his defence of the faith, and we pray for all the faithful departed.
We ask your blessing upon friends and loved ones departed, and pray especially for . . .
Merciful Father,
accept these prayers for the sake of your Son, our Saviour, Jesus Christ.
Amen.

The peace

God give you grace to rejoice in his presence,
to know his love,
and to abide in his peace.
The peace of the Lord be always with you.
And also with you.

Blessing

The love of God draw you to himself,
the power of God strengthen you in his service,
the peace of God be in your hearts and homes:
and the blessing of God Almighty, the Father, the Son and the Holy Spirit, be upon you and remain with you always.
Amen.

8 DECEMBER

The Conception of the Blessed Virgin Mary

This festival celebrating the conception of the mother of Jesus is celebrated in both the Eastern and Western Church on this day. The feast began in the seventh century and was to celebrate God's purpose of love for humankind. It celebrates that humankind can be the bearer of God, and that our God is not a God far off but can be found within us and about us. We are all called by God's grace to bring his presence to be known in the world.

Readings

Genesis 3:9-15, 20
Ephesians 1:3-6, 11, 12
Luke 1:26-38

Opening prayer

O God, in the willingness of the Blessed Virgin Mary, you were able to reveal your love for us and your presence that is with us. We give you thanks for the parents and ancestors of Mary, for without them Mary would not have been born. We pray that we may be open to your presence in our lives and reveal your glory in the world: we ask this in the love of Jesus Christ, our Lord.

Intercessions

Loving God, as we give thanks for the Blessed Virgin Mary, her parents and all her ancestors, we pray for the Jewish people and their rich heritage.
We pray for all who have shared their faith with us and those who have taught us of your love.

We pray for the family of the Church throughout the world and remember those who are suffering for their faith.
Lord, as we have received an awareness of you, may we seek to share this awareness by the way we live and hand our faith on to others.
Lord, your will be done in us,
that we may reveal your love.

Loving God, we pray for all expectant mothers, for maternity hospitals, and for those who will give birth to their children without the provisions of medical care.
We pray for all who act as midwives and all who help to bring new life into the world.
We ask your blessing upon all organisations that seek to uphold family life, and the preciousness and uniqueness of each individual.
Lord, may we respect the preciousness of life in every creature.
Lord, your will be done in us,
that we may reveal your love.

Loving God, we give thanks for our parents and ancestors and pray for all who have made our lives possible.
We ask your blessing upon our loved ones, our homes and the communities to which we belong.
We pray for children taken into care, for those who feel unloved and unwanted, and those who have suffered from violent homes.
We remember families torn apart through war, and pray for those who do not know where they belong or who will care for them.
Lord, your will be done in us,
that we may reveal your love.

Loving God, we pray for those who have lost a child through illness or accident, for the healing of their sorrow and help in their pain.
We pray for couples that would like to have a family, but are unable.
We ask your blessing upon all who are left without relatives and who are lonely and anxious about their future.
We pray for all who are ill or distressed in any way, and we pray for those who are dear to us suffering in any way.
Lord, your will be done in us,
that we may reveal your love.

Loving God, we give you thanks for the faith handed on from generation to generation, and for all your faithful people.
We give thanks especially today for the Blessed Virgin Mary and for her parents.
We remember before you our loved ones and friends who are departed from us . . .
May they rejoice in the fullness of eternal life.
Merciful Father,
accept these prayers for the sake of your Son, our Saviour, Jesus Christ.
Amen.

The peace

The Lord is always with you;
in his presence is the fullness of joy,
and abiding peace.
The peace of the Lord be always with you.
And also with you.

Blessing

God, who created you out of love, is all around you.
Christ who redeemed you by his love, is with you.
The Spirit of God within you fill you with his love:
and the blessing of God Almighty, the Father, the Son and the Holy Spirit, be upon you and remain with you always.
Amen.

13 DECEMBER

Lucy

Lucy was probably born in Syracuse, which is in Sicily. As a young Christian, she dedicated her life to the love of Christ and did not want to marry. She resisted the advances of a pagan suitor. It was probably because of this that she was betrayed to the authorities, then arrested, tortured and killed during the Diocletian persecutions about the year 304. Due to her name, which means 'light', being remembered near the shortest day of the year, she is associated with the festival of light, especially in Sweden.

Readings

Wisdom 3:1-7
2 Corinthians 4:6-15
Matthew 25:1-13

Opening prayer

God of light and love, as we give you thanks for Lucy, may the light of Christ shine in our hearts and homes, so that we reveal your presence and glory in our lives and actions: we ask this in the love of Christ, our Lord.

Intercessions

God of light and life, as we rejoice in this day, may we live in the light of your presence and know the fire of your love.
We give you thanks and praise for the witness of Lucy and remember the many Christians who are still being imprisoned, tortured or put to death for their faith.
We pray for the Church and people of Sicily, and for the Church in Sweden as it celebrates the Festival of Light.

Lord, may your Church work to reveal your light to all lives and nations that walk in darkness.
Light of Christ,
shine within us and through us.

God of light and life, we give you thanks for all who are shining lights in the world and who dedicate themselves to the service of others.
We remember those who care for the needy and the oppressed, often at risk to their own lives.
We pray for those who care for the conservation of our world and for the preservation of species.
We pray for all who reveal your love and peace, and ask your blessing upon the work of the United Nations and all who negotiate for harmony between nations.
Light of Christ,
shine within us and through us.

God of light and life, we give thanks for those who have brought light and love to our lives and ask your blessing upon our friends and loved ones.
We pray for all who supply our homes with power, light and water, and remember in our prayers homes and families that do not have easy access to these resources.
We pray for families that are struggling with some darkness in their lives and live in fear of the future.
We give thanks for and ask your blessing upon all care workers and the social services: may we be of help to others wherever we can.
Light of Christ,
shine within us and through us.

God of light and life, we remember those lives that are darkened by depression and doubt.
We pray for those who live in fear for their lives, for all who have lost homes or loved ones.
We pray for all who are ill, injured or suffer from a disability, those who are afflicted in any way.
We remember friends and loved ones who are in need or in sickness . . .
Light of Christ,
shine within us and through us.

God of light and life, we pray for all who are in the shadow of death
and for their loved ones in their sorrow.
We give thanks for Lucy and all who rejoice in the fullness of light
eternal.
We ask your blessing upon friends and loved ones who are departed . . .
Merciful Father,
accept these prayers for the sake of your Son, our Saviour, Jesus Christ.
Amen.

The peace

God, in whom you trust, enlighten your life
and fill you with all joy and peace in believing.
The peace of the Lord be always with you.
And also with you.

Blessing

God, the creator of light, enfold you;
Christ, the light of the world, uphold you;
the Holy Spirit, enlightening all people, be with you:
and the blessing of God Almighty, the Father, the Son and the Holy
Spirit, be upon you and remain with you always.
Amen.

14 DECEMBER

John of the Cross

John of the Cross was born in 1542 of an impoverished noble family at Fontiveros near Avila in Spain. He was brought up by a widowed mother and educated at a charity school. He worked as a nurse and received further education from the Jesuits and was professed by them. At the age of 21, he left and joined the Carmelites in Madeira and studied theology in Salamanca. In 1567 he was ordained priest and soon afterwards met Teresa of Avila for the first time. It was Teresa who persuaded John to lead the reformed Discalced Carmelites. She had been given two houses for friars to further this purpose, and John became the head of one of these houses. Not all the brethren were keen on his reforms and John suffered many trials and tribulations, including being imprisoned at Toledo for nine months in 1575. After ten years of being Superior of various houses, John fell out of favour and was banished to Andalusia in southern Spain where he died of a severe illness in 1591. John was a mystic and poet, a man of great honesty and prayer. He wrote a great deal on the mystery of the cross and of his own *Dark Night of the Soul*, which he began while in prison.

Readings

1 Kings 19:9-18
1 Corinthians 2:1-10
John 14:18-23

Opening prayer

God, who gave to your priest John of the Cross a love of Christ crucified and the faith to conquer the darkness and doubt that sought to overcome him, grant us an awareness of your presence and love with us always, even when it is dark and troubles surround us: we ask this in the name of Christ, who died upon the cross for us.

Intercessions

God of grace and goodness, we pray for the Church in Spain, and for the Carmelites and the Jesuits.
As we give thanks for John of the Cross, we remember those who suffer trials and tribulations for their faith and those who are imprisoned.
We give thanks for the writings of John of the Cross and pray for poets, authors and those who show their faith to us through words and actions.
We ask that we and the whole Church may witness to your presence, no matter how dark the day or life is.
Lighten our darkness,
Lord, we pray.

God of grace and goodness, we pray for all who live in areas of violence or conflict, especially those whose lives are endangered.
We ask your blessing upon all who work to bring peace and unity to our world whilst respecting the diversity of people and nations.
We pray for all who seek to free those who are unjustly imprisoned, and we pray for the work of Amnesty International.
Lord, grant us an awareness of your love for all of your creation, and may we reveal that love by the way we live.
Lighten our darkness,
Lord, we pray.

God of grace and goodness, we give thanks for all who bring light and joy into our lives and pray for our loved ones and friends.
We pray for communities and families that are breaking up and for the upheaval it is causing to all.
We remember areas where old wounds and animosities are still felt strongly and pray for their healing.
We ask your blessing upon all who seek to provide decent homes and places of shelter for all who are made homeless.
Lighten our darkness,
Lord, we pray.

God of grace and goodness, we pray for those who are confused or distressed by the changes taking place around them and in their lives.
We remember all who are struggling due to failure of crops, poverty and hunger, and ask your blessing upon all trying to help them.

We pray for those whose lives are darkened by fear, depression or doubt.
We pray for all who are ill and for their loved ones in their fears and anxieties: and remember before you friends and loved ones in their troubles . . .
Lighten our darkness,
Lord, we pray.

God of grace and goodness, we give thanks for the light of your love and the gift of eternal life.
We pray for John of the Cross and all your saints who have revealed your presence.
We remember before you our loved ones departed . . .
Merciful Father,
accept these prayers for the sake of your Son, our Saviour, Jesus Christ. Amen.

The peace

God is with you in darkness and in light,
his love upholds you day and night,
his peace surrounds you and never leaves you.
The peace of the Lord be always with you.
And also with you.

Blessing

God the Creator deliver you from all evil,
Christ of the Cross and resurrection be your light,
the Holy Spirit be your strength and your peace:
and the blessing of God Almighty, the Father, the Son and the Holy Spirit, be upon you and remain with you always.
Amen.

29 DECEMBER

Thomas Becket

Thomas was born of a wealthy Norman family at Cheapside in London in 1118. He was educated at Merton College and in Paris. He became a financial clerk for a while and was then invited to join the curia of Theobald, Archbishop of Canterbury. He was sent to study law at Bologna and Auxerre. After being ordained deacon in 1154, he became the Archdeacon of Canterbury. He was so capable in this position that Theobald used him to negotiate with the Crown. When Henry II became King, he chose Becket to be the Chancellor of England in 1155. In the beginning, he had a very good relationship with the King. Expecting this to continue, in 1162 Henry obtained Becket's election as Archbishop of Canterbury. Unexpectedly Becket went through a conversion, living an austere way of life and taking his duties as Archbishop seriously. He resigned as Chancellor, much to the annoyance of the King. He opposed Henry in matters of taxation and the claims of secular courts on ecclesiastics for offences already dealt with by the Church. He also demanded when necessary his freedom to appeal to Rome. On appealing to the Pope over Henry's demands for money and for almost standing alone against the King, he was forced to flee in to exile in France in 1164. He remained in France for six years. During this time his lands in England were confiscated by the King and Becket's supporters persecuted; relations worsened. Then in 1170, during a temporary reconciliation, Becket returned to Canterbury. However, there were soon new conflicts between these two powerful men. In a rage Henry said to his courtiers, 'Who will rid me of this turbulent priest?' Four barons took Henry at his word and, after an altercation with Becket, killed him in his own cathedral. Becket died in 1170, commending his cause to God. Thomas became the patron saint of pastoral clergy in England and Wales.

Readings

Ecclesiasticus 51:1-8
2 Timothy 2:8-13; 3:10-12
Matthew 10:28-33

Opening prayer

Lord of life and life eternal, who gave your servant Thomas Becket the courage to stand firm in what he believed was right in defending the Church, grant us your grace to be firm in our faith and to stand against all evil: we ask this in the name of Christ, our Saviour.

Intercessions

Holy and Almighty God, as we give thanks for Thomas Becket, we pray for Canterbury Cathedral, for *(name)* the Archbishop of Canterbury and for all who live within the diocese and province.
We ask your blessing upon the worldwide Communion of the Anglican Church and pray that it may be an instrument of unity and peace.
We pray for those who are being imprisoned, tortured or put to death for their faith, and for all whose lives are endangered.
We pray for all who are new to the faith and those who will nurture and be a strength to them.
Good Shepherd, hear us,
guide us and help us.

Holy and Almighty God, we ask your blessing upon Elizabeth our Queen and all the royal family.
We pray for our government and for good relations between Church and state.
We remember all who risk their lives to protect our environment and who stand against large multinationals that are exploiting the earth's resources.
We give thanks and pray for all who defend our freedom, maintain our peace, and strive for fair dealing for all people.
Good Shepherd, hear us,
guide us and help us.

Holy and Almighty God, we give you thanks for the comfort and protection of our homes and ask your blessing upon our loved ones and friends.
We give thanks for all who have taught us, and ask your blessing upon the schools and colleges of our area.
We pray for families who are struggling, where there is little or no employment and where people are deeply in debt.

We pray for all who enrich our lives through art, music, writings and entertainments.
Good Shepherd, hear us,
guide us and help us.

Holy and Almighty God, we remember all who have suffered through acts of tyranny, violence or war.
We pray for families who have been made homeless, those who have lost loved ones, and all who suffer from hunger.
We remember those who are struggling with illness, infirmity or disease, and those who are anxious about their future.
We remember friends and loved ones in need or in illness . . .
Good Shepherd, hear us,
guide us and help us.

Holy and Almighty God, we give thanks for all who have revealed your love and glory to the world, for all your saints.
We give thanks for Thomas Becket and his witnessing to his faith.
We pray for all the faithful departed, and remember especially . . .
Merciful Father,
accept these prayers for the sake of your Son, our Saviour, Jesus Christ.
Amen.

The peace

Let God be your hope, your guide, your strength
and your peace today and every day.
The peace of the Lord be always with you.
And also with you.

Blessing

The presence of the Almighty protect you;
the peace of Christ the Saviour be upon you;
the power of the Holy Spirit be your strength:
and the blessing of God Almighty, the Father, the Son and the Holy Spirit, be upon you and remain with you always.
Amen.